Contents

Cover design and Layout by S.Y Lee-Wan
Editing and Publishing by Jen Hayes
Interview editing and Proofing by Meghan Worley

ISBN: 978-1-7331346-9-9

Dedication

Jenny, Ben, Ana, Mia, and Aubrey —
I am a lucky guy to have all of you in my life.

To my Dad —
I miss you and wish I could have shared this with you.
You taught me early in my life that leading is a choice
and not a title.

To the amazing leaders I get to work with and learn from —
The EOS® Journey is what we do,
but your passion and drive to be great inspires me.
Thanks for the trust by inviting me to be your partner.

My team —
Emily, Jen, Shuk-Yee, Meghan, and Craig.
I would not have tried to complete this without you.
Thank you for saying 'Yes' when I asked for your help.

Thank you Diana, Donna, Javier, Paul, Rick, and Jane
for sharing your wisdom and allowing me
to shine a spotlight on you!

Honest Culture Journey™

Preface

Maya Angelou once said, "A bird doesn't sing because it has an answer, it sings because it has a song."

I wrote this book for the same reason I wrote my first book, *People-Centered Performance* – I have a passion for maximizing growth and minimizing pain, helping people move to and past the tipping point of success. I am also a guide at heart; I like to walk with people.

I have walked what I call the Honest Culture Journey many times as a husband, father, brother, son, friend, coach, consultant, and EOS Implementer™. When I looked back at what worked and what didn't work (and when it doesn't work, there is very real pain), I realized I could create a simple map to help navigate this journey. I intentionally use the word journey – the Honest Culture Journey – to constantly remind my fellow travelers what we are preparing for.

I originally put pen to paper in 2014, and much has happened since then. One of the most significant changes for me has been my work as an EOS Implementer™, through which I have spent hundreds of days working with leadership teams and watching relational things like trust and honesty interact with individual entrepreneurial spirit. Between days with leadership teams, individual conversations, time with boards, workshops, and conversations after keynotes, the time I've spent learning and observing is into the thousands of hours. The most significant outcome of all this work is a set of unwavering beliefs – in the impact of great leaders, the core desire of most people to be great at their job, and the crucial role honesty plays in the two critical success factors for teams: clarity and alignment.

This book is for leaders who want to build a team that performs at a high level and develop a culture that will be the glue for continued success. If your single goal is the next round of funding, climbing over your peers to get a bigger title, or a 4-hour work week – this book is probably not for you. I don't say that to diminish the importance of those goals; I say it because at the core of the Honest Culture Journey is an African proverb I use often:

If you want to go fast, go alone.
If you want to go far, go together.

99

Another quote I have heard lately is:

Sometimes you have to slow down in order to speed up.

99

I like to practice what I preach. For me, to slow down and listen meant committing to interview a group of leaders so that I could bring other voices to you. This evolved into a plan to ultimately interview 25 to 30 leaders, with at least 50% of those leaders being women or of color, so that you could listen in on a conversation with a leader that you might connect with because of their background or their voice.

I have so far completed six of these interviews – and I underestimated how transforming they would be for me. These six interviews have challenged my thinking and completely energized me with their different perspectives on the Honest Culture Journey. I also felt humbled by friends who were so willing to give of their time because they value our relationship. One of my values is Kindness Matters, and it was good to be reminded that when we focus on what matters to us, good things will happen..

In this book, you will have the company of six leaders who are great at what they do. As you get to know them, I hope you are inspired to find your own voice and courage to take this journey.

For those of you ready to go on this journey,
thank you for joining me.

Introduction

Building an Honest Culture through relationships

*Leadership is working with people
to accomplish their goals and the
goals of the organization.*

Ken Blanchard

The Honest Culture Journey is built on relationships.

We have all had relationships that have frustrated us.
Do any of these situations feel familiar?

- You are a member of a team on which there is someone who says yes to everything. You cringe when it's something you need, because you have zero confidence it will get done.

- Everyone on the team sees the elephant in the room, so why doesn't someone just name it? Ever since that big issue started going unaddressed, lots of 'little elephants' like missed deadlines, conflict between sales and production, and customer issues have started hanging around. What's everyone afraid of?

- Every time you're in a meeting with them, they dismiss your ideas or argue with you. Their priorities are so different from yours, and they make you feel like an idiot.

- You hired a new team member, but the busyness of work has kept you from onboarding them well. They are three months into employment and you're just not comfortable with letting them work independently. They also don't seem to be connecting well with the team.

- You love your team meetings, but nothing happens in between. The bar for performance seems to be getting lower and it is frustrating. How do you fix it? Is it possible to have high accountability while keeping that supportive and fun culture?

- You love challenging work, but lately you've started thinking that it's only a matter of time before everyone sees through your veneer and realizes you are a fraud. That word 'fraud' bugs you, but lately you're spending a lot of energy putting on a happy, confident face – and that is energy taken away from doing your work.

This list could equally have ventured into the relationship dynamics we experience in our neighborhoods, the boards we serve on, and with any community project we take on .

> *Wherever work is getting done and relationships exist,*
> *there is a culture.*
>
> *Scott Patchin*

99

We might not think about it, but it is there. Imagine if all those situations were charged with honesty, performance, and love?

Did I catch you off guard with that word: 'love'? In my first book, *People-Centered Performance,* I shared my belief that *fear motivates in the short term, but love motivates in the long term.* The love I speak of was given to us by the ancient Greeks, who had four words for love. While Eros was centered around sexual passion, Agape is a word referring to selfless passion. It is that selfless love that makes teams healthy: where we are able to speak the truth to others, and – more importantly – hear the truth from others. All the situations above need a dose of honest culture to evolve into situations that **build** relationships and performance instead of eroding them.

If any of these situations resonate with you, and you are ready for the personal change that is critical to a successful journey, then let's look at the map that will help us navigate.

Reading the map

On a recent trip in an unfamiliar town, my wife was at the helm of Google Maps. We missed two different turns because *Google was too slow*. I love my wife, and yet there were times when I just wanted to say that I need a navigator to help me make the right turns when I'm at them – not after I have passed. As a 27-year veteran of marriage, I did not do that for obvious reasons. One reason was it had done the same thing to me many times when I was both driver and navigator. But with a *safe* journey as the goal, it was equally important to be patient with both my wife and Google to achieve this. Maps are not foolproof yet understanding how they can be used effectively as tools, despite their limitations, helps us arrive safely and still be married!

Moving toward an Honest Culture is a journey. Therefore, we have a map (below) to help us navigate this journey. This should help you see the steps needed and give you a clear view of our destination.

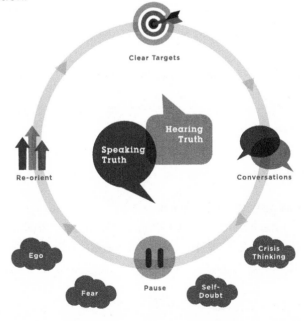

Packing your bags

In preparation for the journey ahead, chapter 1 will lay the foundation and outline some key things you need to bring on this journey. Remember that 100% preparation is not the point, but I will share the most important things to bring. Ignoring my advice will just make your journey harder. If the goal is a healthy (pain minimized) and successful end, it might take you a couple of times around the circle before you and your team feel like announcing, "We're here!"

The reality is, in business, we often have to start a journey without all the necessary things. Waiting until you have all four items I outline firmly in place is often not realistic. My best advice is that if you feel they are forgotten, and you are the leader of the team, just tell your team, apologize, and make a plan to address any problems you may encounter proactively. Remember, transparency builds trust!

After the foundation in chapter 1, we'll take a deep dive into each step in chapters 2, 3, 4, and 5.

But first, here are four things you need to remember when reading this map:

1. No skipping steps:

Each step is its own item and doing each one well sets the stage for the next step.

2. Thou shalt always go forward:

We never go backward; we just sometimes move forward through a few steps more quickly. This is designed to create discipline and success, not bureaucracy!

3. Participation in each step will vary; ownership won't:
The participants in each step will be different, which I will explain in more detail throughout the upcoming chapters. As leaders, we want our team members to own this journey for themselves and the team.

4. Clouds = barriers to our success:
These are the negative feelings that can obstruct our view of the targets we set and derail us from our journey. Clouds will be addressed at every step.

Let me repeat a critical point: this is designed to create discipline, momentum, and success, not bureaucracy.

Speaking truth about the journey
Let's recognize the tension having a map can create because of the varied personalities of all those involved. Some of you are planners, so a map excites you and automatically connects with your gift to plan. You are also likely to fall into the trap that sees any resistance to the plan as reckless; you will not trust anyone working without a plan. When insisting on a lot of detail or long discussions around the plan, there will be conflict with the entrepreneurial-minded leader on your team that only really sees the arrows and wants to get started on the work now.

I have named the tension, and we will return often to this theme as we move ahead. This will have a significant impact on our ability to build this honest culture and achieve all the great outcomes we want for our teams and organization.

I can't solve this for you, but by speaking the truth about these tensions, you will be able to step back from this map on occasion and focus on the central speak truth / hear truth mandate!

The last idea I would like to sew with you is something that was shared with me that had a significant impact on how I view this journey. It is contained in a quote that I included on the cover of this book.

The opposite of truth is not a lie.

Dr. Donna Lowry

99

I am not going to unpack this idea with you right now because some things require time to consider. It deepens the meaning, and often pulls us into other conversations as we struggle with the feelings they generate in us. Becoming a great leader is not a fast journey, but a far journey. So let's spend some time walking this part together.

Chapter 1

Setting the stage for the Honest Culture Journey
Creating context for our conversation

*Working hard for something we don't care about
is called stress.
Working hard for something we love
is called passion.*

Simon Sinek

If your goal is great performance outcomes and a positive culture with strong relationships, then the steps are clear:

- **Clear Targets:** Work with your team to set targets, so your desired outcomes are clear and focused.

- **Conversations:** Be present and attentive for all the interactions that occur daily as you live and work. This allows you to display a great sense for what is unsaid as well as what is said.

- **Pause:** Conduct meetings purposefully and strategically, making sure there is time to both listen and talk, and using honesty to drive the result of team clarity. You should see and feel the presence of 90 to 100% transparency.

- **Re-orient:** Prioritize and act upon what is shared in the Pause. Any changes to key assumptions and plans should be either reinforced or revised. This sends your relationships back to where we started with Clear Targets.

The overall goal of all your Conversations, no matter how short, is speaking and hearing truth.

The enemies of honesty, which you must manage to participate effectively in these Conversations, are:

These are the clouds that can settle in on your journey and impact your success along with that of your team. Generally these clouds reduce our ability to listen to each other, create artificial 'immediate' deadlines, and generate stories in our own heads that become reality to us yet are a mystery to everyone around us – because 95% of them are not true.

Insights in Leadership

Paul Doyle

If speaking the truth becomes code for giving hard feedback, maybe we've missed the point. Speaking the truth can equally be: "That was awesome. That's an incredible success. I really appreciate what you just got done." So speaking the truth...maybe we need to elevate it. Regardless of whether it's good, bad, or neutral, the purpose of speaking the truth is to serve. If I want to embolden you, give you some positive feedback, speak that truth – the purpose for me to do that is to reinforce or to encourage or to appreciate. If it's something that has to be hard, then speaking the truth is, if it comes from my heart: "I want to help. I want you to be better."

Truth *Insights in Leadership*

Dr. Donna Lowry

First of all, the assumption that the opposite of truth is a lie is a barrier. I think it's a misnomer that truth is pure and crystal clear. It's almost like – truth is good, not-truth is bad, or the truth will be obvious. When we ingrain the belief that *the opposite of truth is not a lie* into our brain, this barrier loses its power.

Let me provide a brief description of each so you can determine if any of them are impacting you or your team right now.

Ego: Ego by itself is neutral and possessed by everyone. The definition of ego is simply the opinion that you have about yourself. However, the higher you climb in an organization, the more pressure there is to become unshakable and to produce results.

This can result in an inflated ego which acts to devalue the opinions of others, funnels energy into looking good, and has the need to always be 'in charge', just to name a few. This undermines every step of the Honest Culture Journey because it blocks the ability of the person with the inflated Ego and everyone around them to speak and hear truth.

Fear: We all worry. If you wrote down the top 10 things you were worried about right now, how many of those things do you think will happen? The number is 5%, so at least nine on your list are just consuming your mental energy. I learned this one firsthand when I was part of an organization that reduced staff every fall for seven years. It was extra damaging because each event had a kind of cumulative effect. I did not really notice the impact until I left the organization and joined an entrepreneurial company where we focused on possibilities and opportunities.

When our fears drive our actions, we are only able to hear truth in bits and pieces, if at all. Most of our energy is focused on processing the honesty of the people sharing information and calculating how honest we should be. Ever been there?

Insights in Leadership

Diana J. Wong, PhD

In myself and in working with many people, the greatest hesitancy in speaking truth is not valuing truth more than fear. It's:

• Fear of what other people may think

• Fear that they don't like me

• Fear of the negative consequences that are imagined

Some of them can be real, but often we project the consequences. I find fear to be a great barrier to truth. When it's a truth-telling moment, when it's really important, and when the stakes are really high, one has to have courage to confront one's own fears, battle them, and wrestle them to the ground. Often times it's not enough to go to it alone. This is where I call on my army of support.

Courage is resistance to fear, mastery of fear
– not absence of fear.

Mark Twain

99

Insights in Leadership

Dr. Donna Lowry

Fear is limbic. It's really primal, and it gets in the way of our cognitive processing. The challenge with spotting fear is that it's pretty nuanced. That makes it hard to spot, and puts the culture at risk because someone responding and acting out of fear can ruin a culture. The advice I would give new leaders is to focus on asking questions, listening really well, and where possible, do some scenario planning because that makes it harder for fear to hide.

 Self-doubt: Have you ever left a meeting feeling like a fraud because it seemed like everyone had something to add while you just sat there? You wonder how long it will be before someone questions why you are even there. This is a close relative of ego and fear because it is born from a fragile or low ego that is magnified by the presence of fear in our head. All of these push decision-making to the lizard brain (amygdala) where our choices become fight or flight. Flight is most often the answer, restricting our ability to speak truth and hear truth. The net impact is to slow us down so the journey goes on without us or someone has to spend extra effort to carry us.

The first part of our brain, the part that shows up first in the womb, the part that was there a million years ago – that's our lizard brain. The lizard brain is in charge of fight or flight, of anger, and of survival. That's all we used to need, and even now, when there's an emergency, the lizard brain is still in charge.

There are several small parts of your brain near the end of your spinal cord responsible for survival and other wild-animal traits. The whole thing is called the basal ganglia, and there are two almond shaped bits in everyone's brain. Scientists call these the amygdala, and this mini-brain apparently takes over whenever you are angry, afraid, aroused, hungry, or in search of revenge. (Seth Godin, *Linchpin: Are You Indispensable?* p108-109)

 Crisis thinking: Have you ever rushed to get something done because of a deadline, only to be told that things had changed and you had a couple hours, days, or maybe even weeks left? Maybe just because it came from your bosses' boss you thought it was needed now. Crisis thinking is just that, and when we are in it decision-making gets faster, collaboration decreases, and we cut corners on things like data, testing, and proofing. Like the other three clouds, crisis thinking acts to impede the speaking and hearing of truth. For a leader, the excuse becomes 'not enough time' to discuss it. Most often, this is a self-generated myth.

For each step in the Honest Culture Journey, I want to have a cloud discussion. It is important for you as the leader to be aware that all these feelings exist within yourself and your team. Your job is to be alert to seeing them when they show up, and to display the courage and vulnerability to name and discuss them.

Courage can be learned if we're willing to put down our armor and pick up the shared language, tools, and skills we need for rumbling with vulnerability, living into our values, braving trust, and learning to rise.

Brené Brown, Dare to Lead

99

As I was interviewing leaders for this book, one leader stepped back and offered a different view of the clouds by translating all the cloud-generating behaviors to cloud-dissipating behaviors.

Insights in Leadership

Diana J. Wong, PhD

For each one of these, there should be a parallel of the positive. I view these clouds as potholes in the journey, and challenge leaders to reframe them into behaviors that will fill them in or not allow them to develop in the first place.

• Positive to ego is self-confidence

• Positive to fear is courage

• Positive to self-doubt is purpose

> **Note on purpose:** The idea is about a purpose-driven leader. When you're clear about your purpose you don't have to question whether your idea is good enough. If Amanda's sense-of-self is that she has a really science-y mind and is really brilliant in science, she doesn't have to go into all the detail to prove her opinion. When I coached her, a challenge is that she over-informs in order to speak to upper level leaders. By swamping them with information, they get confused, and she sabotages herself and diminishes her impact. You have to do it in concise, clear messages, then allow them to ask the questions. You always anchor yourself in purpose.

• Positive to crisis thinking is presence

Note on presence: Presence and planning go together in my mind. Let's use the pandemic as an example. We're all in a crisis about it, but there has been a playbook for it that has been practiced multiple times over by officials at local, state, and federal levels. Knowing that we're in a crisis actually clears up crisis thinking. If you know that you're in a crisis, there are well-written scripts on how to manage a crisis. There are many well-written scripts for what leaders need to do in a crisis. So inform yourself, rely on experts that can move you out of crisis thinking, and allow yourself to have presence as a leader.

One additional comment on the conversation we are about to have: be cautious of simple. The intellectual understanding of the Honest Culture Journey will be the easy part. As you go out and practice it, the work will provide some powerful, emotionally charged moments for all those involved, and some of them will be hard. That is why we are travelling together.

Simple is rarely easy. Especially when it involves things like trust, conflict, love, truth, and teamwork.

Scott Patchin

In the movie *Up and Away*, George Clooney played a self-obsessed consultant who had a side job as a motivational speaker. In his spiel, he used the analogy of packing a bag to equip people to go out and have a more successful life.

That analogy works here too, because this is a journey. By definition, this is *an act or instance of traveling from one place to another.* When we travel, we are compelled to bring things with us that we will need at the next place.

My first book contained a leader's packing list for our Honest Culture Journey. Here are the four most important things to bring:

Item #1: Clarity on your beliefs about leadership, people, and relationships

Here are mine:

- Great conversations start with a question

- Honest conversations are the foundation of great relationships

- Leadership is working with people

- Fear motivates only for the short term, but love motivates for the long term

- Everyone has the potential to be amazing at a job

- Individuals own development; organizations own support

- In great organizations, everyone leads

- Trust is a gift

- A, B, and C players exist in all organizations

These beliefs direct my actions, and cause guilt and procrastination when they are violated. They become filters for the words and actions of others, and when unchecked, will cause me to make quick judgements on the actions of others.

We judge ourselves based on our intent.
We judge others based on their actions.
Stephen M.R. Covey, *Speed of Trust*

99

The hard truth is that clear beliefs and the ability to live by those beliefs, regardless of the circumstances, becomes a foundation for wisdom, character, and trustworthiness.

Wisdom – a wise attitude, belief, or course of action.
Ability to discern inner qualities and relationships.
Merriam-Webster.com

99

What are your core beliefs? Undertaking this journey without these identified will make some of the tough decisions even harder. By defining them, you start on your journey to wisdom. Defining your core beliefs also allows others to see into your heart and mind. With this transparency, you equip your fellow travelers to understand the intent behind your actions.

Item #2: A clear and objective view of yourself
Know thyself. The negative impact of defining your beliefs is that upon closer examination by others, you almost instantly become identified as a hypocrite.

Hypocrite – A person who acts in contradiction to his or her stated beliefs or feelings. The word hypocrisy comes from the Greek ὑπόκρισις (hypokrisis), which means 'jealous', 'play-acting', 'acting out', 'coward', or 'dissembling'.

One great challenge of being a leader is that you are judged by the perceptions of those you lead – and we all know that our perceptions become our reality. Being able to step back to see our actions through a set of guiding beliefs and having a willingness to receive feedback from others is called vulnerability.

A tool I use with leaders to explore this dynamic is called the Johari Window. It helps us view our interpersonal relationships through two lenses: what we know and don't know about ourselves, and what others know and don't know about us (see below).

	KNOWN TO SELF	UNKNOWN TO SELF
KNOWN TO OTHERS	OPEN	BLIND SPOT
UNKNOWN TO OTHERS	HIDDEN	UNKNOWN

This tool can be used to help surface some of the perceptions that others have of you as a leader.

In the Johari Window, something others see or perceive about us and we don't see is called a blind spot. Once, when I was leading a team, I had the chance to get some feedback from all of them and one of the key messages was that I was not delegating effectively to them. In their view, I was trying to do too much myself. I saw myself just the opposite at the time, so that was a blind spot. The

Conversations I had with the team afterwards helped to move that into the open area; I was then able to make some changes as a leader to get them more involved in our work by delegating more effectively. As a simple rule for eliminating blind spots and moving things into the open frame – we just need to ask. We repeat that action over and over by having regular Conversations that invite others to share their perceptions, which is their truth, with us. The outcome for us as leaders is to create a real-time clear and objective view of ourselves.

If you want to learn more about the Johari Window and how it can help you as a leader, here is a short video I created to support your journey. *(https://youtu.be/ofs7oBquODg)*

 Truth ———— *Insights in Leadership* ————

Jane Clark

Something I haven't talked about is that I am so competitive, and it's hard for me to turn it off. I trace that back to the reading competition in first grade. I'll catch myself because I want to turn everything into a game or a competition. If we just did an event, I'll say, "What do you think our net promoter scores are going to be? Or what's your goal for the number of people that are going to come?" I like winning. Finding that balance is important, because this is not all about me. One thing I have learned is that instead of focusing on turning it off, I acknowledge it and my team acknowledges it. It's just who I am. The outcome of this is I see my team willing to challenge my ideas or explore the questions I put out there instead of getting defensive. The impact on me is that the work I have been doing for 20+ years still energizes me.

Item #3: Trust established to x%

> *Trust does not necessarily mean that I like you,*
> *it means I understand you.*
>
> *Peter Drucker*

99

In Patrick Lencioni's iconic business book, *The Five Dysfunctions of a Team,* he makes the following points about trust:

> *Trust lies at the heart of a functioning, cohesive team.*
> *Without it, teamwork is all but impossible.*

99

> *In the context of building a team, trust is the confidence*
> *among team members that their peers' intentions are good,*
> *and that there is no reason to be protective or careful around the*
> *group. In essence, teammates must get comfortable being*
> *vulnerable with one another. (p.195)*

99

While trust can and will be built during a well-travelled Honest Culture Journey, having some built before the work starts makes a positive outcome more assured. At the center of the journey is speaking truth and hearing truth. For people to speak it, they have to trust those around them enough to:

- Challenge their leader

- Accept input without ego

- Provide input to their peers

Item #4: Clear relationship context

My first job was with a bankrupt steel company, and as you can imagine, the culture of the organization was toxic. I liked the people I worked with, but there was a prevailing us versus them mentality and lots of individual survival behavior. I was young, and I thought all work was probably like that. It was not until my next job that I got to experience a culture where the goal was to succeed as a team. It was an 'aha' moment for me.

The goal of this journey is to have stronger relationships at the end of the project or fiscal year than existed at the beginning. This goal makes things like transparency, honesty, hearing each other, clear commitments, and exploring why things *don't* get done critical behaviors that we must all practice. Let me stress again – this journey is all about RELATIONSHIPS, because it involves more than one person working together effectively to reach a desired outcome AND strengthening the relationship in the process. Remember my core belief that *leadership is working with people* and *honest conversations are the foundation of great relationships.*

Let me share some examples of how clarifying the context of our relationships before we take a journey together lays a foundation for a smoother, healthier journey – where trust is built, and healthy conflict happens when needed:

- **Boss to employee:**
  The context of this relationship is centered around work styles, the expectations of what each needs from the other, and the ability to build things like trust and respect during the ups and downs that happen in any relationship. A foundation of trust starts with:

  1. What do you expect from me? [as your leader]

2. What do you expect from me? [as your employee]

3. What are the two or three key things you need from me so that in 2 months you can feel that your trust in me has increased?

4. How are we going to stay on the same page around priorities, key decisions, and problems that need to be solved (including by when)?

Truth ——— *Insights in Leadership* ———

Rick Baker

I feel like there's a couple of ways that people approach others with regard to trust. The first is they are like my late grandfather. His approach was he didn't trust anyone. They had to earn it. I am actually the opposite. I think everyone starts with what I call your trust account. It's like a bank account. With him, everyone's bank account is sort of empty. The bigger your account got, the more he trusted you. I start everyone with a full trust account, but you only get a couple withdrawals. I don't know if either one is right or wrong. I think it's just people's approach to how they trust people or not.

Truth ——— *Insights in Leadership* ———

Dr. Donna Lowry

Personally, and it is probably my medical background emerging, I definitely have a habit of trust and verification, but trust first. One critical step is setting aside your assumptions of who or what is trustworthy. As an example, is somebody with a felony record worthy of trust? I know it is kind of an extreme example and I've never hired somebody with a felony record, but why not? If we give some support around whatever they're doing, they could be successful. That will only happen if we intentionally set aside our assumptions of who or what is trustworthy.

A second critical step is providing clear direction and creating clarity about the role and scope of the role as a key part of building trust. Following this up with being available when people run into tough patches – to partner with them in working through challenges – is important. It gets back to that basic rhythm of trust and verify.

- **Peer to peer:**
  This is similar to the boss to employee relationship, in that work styles, professional and life priorities, and how we will work together are foundational parts of a strong start. With peers, it is also critical to define how you will manage the common situations that come up when two smart, experienced, ego-possessing people go on the Honest Culture Journey. What will you do when you disagree, a deadline is missed, someone is struggling and not asking for help, or when a sacrifice for the greater good of the organization has to be made? A good place to start is sharing the answers to the four basic questions used for the boss to peer relationship.

- **Married couple:**
  You thought this was just about working relationships? That is my focus, but the things we learn to be more effective in our work relationships are the same things that will impact our non-work relationships. If you think back to any pre- or post-marital counseling – or even the ceremony and your vows – they are all about establishing common goals,

making clear commitments, building a clear understanding of each other before the journey starts, and maintaining a clear understanding of each other as we experience personal growth and change during our lives. I also want to be clear that as our laws have updated the definition of marriage to include same-sex couples, I make this point for *all* marriages.

- **Parent to child:**
  This falls into the same area as marriage. The challenge is that the context changes as the child grows. After birth, the context of the relationship changes from one of total dependence to an increasing percentage of independence. In that sense, it is a lot like managing people because as the individual develops their confidence and skills, they need your support as a leader in different ways. I will not cover it specifically in this book, but anything you learn at a parenting seminar that helps you build a healthy and productive relationship with your child will also help in your Honest Culture Journey and vice versa.

  Story to share as a parent: This hit me when my daughter and I both read Lean In by Sheryl Sandberg, and then sat down for lunch to share our thoughts and reactions to it. Selfishly, I wanted to use the time to get to know my adult daughter a little more. She set some context for me when I asked her, "What is the one thing you want me to do that will give you space to be you and strengthen our relationship?" Her response was simple (but not easy for this Dad). She said "Dad, when I share my opinion on something, don't automatically share yours. Just listen for a little while and try to understand why I am saying this." Context is important.

- **Best friend to best friend:**
  We all have a few best friends – those people that we can be transparent with, that we trust with sensitive information about our lives. Yet how often do we create context for what we expect of each other? Sometimes it happens when we dump our emotions on someone, then we apologize and they reassure us with something like, "That's what friends are for. Thanks for trusting me enough to be open." If you look back at your journey with your closest friends, you probably did not necessarily go to a retreat together, but over the years you have established a context for the relationship.

The clouds

Let me identify some common ways that you will hear clouds. You can use this wisdom in every step.

 Ego:

Too much: The Alpha on your team dominates the conversation around how to achieve a goal. When the target or plan is questioned by anyone, the leader or owner of that task shuts down the conversation with a statement like *I got it, let's move on.*

Too little: This will most often show up in the language people use. If you hear statements like *I think, I hope so, kind of, I guess,* or *if I have to* that indicates someone is not confident in themselves.

Insights in Leadership

Javier Olvera

When there is too much ego, it creates an attitude of "This is what I'm entitled to, and this is what I did!" If people want to be recognized as a star, it undermines our family culture that strives for everyone to have a voice and feel equal. As leaders, we work hard to respect people by listening to them, and we hope they follow our lead. This is hard when you are an entrepreneur and want to do things quickly.

Fear:

The conversation around future state involves spoken resistance using adjectives like *crazy* or *impossible* without offering revisions to the target. The other thing that shows up with fear is silence. Silence could also be an issue if you know it is a stretch goal, yet the list of issues or unanswered questions is very short.

Self-doubt:

There is a delayed effect of self-doubt that is hard to really hear in the meeting. Being similar to fear, silence is the greatest indicator. Following up either one-on-one or in a team meeting on the detailed plans behind any targets will also help because self-doubt has a paralyzing effect that will cause people to be unable to put a plan together. Your challenge as a leader is to keep listening for this beyond the planning meeting.

Insights in Leadership

Dr. Donna Lowry

When I hear self-doubt, I believe that empathizing first is important. My typical response might be "You know what? I've felt the same way." Then I would go ahead and describe a scenario I experienced. "This happened to me last Tuesday. This is how I recognized it, and this is how I moved through it." The illustration I share is designed to make it safe for them to see that self-doubt is normal and to create space for them to ask the question, "How do I move through this?" When I see new leaders ask themselves that last question, I know they are going to be okay.

 Crisis Thinking: All the deadlines are tomorrow and/or people put up great resistance to even taking the time to create the target.

 Insights in Leadership

Rick Baker

You can be in crisis thinking even when it's not a crisis if you have the wrong culture. Every day is a crisis if you don't have a team that's going in the same direction or if they're fighting among one another.

Myth: We can push through anything we encounter:
Remember that it is expensive to have to revisit decisions or to create plans that don't accurately address the obvious risks of our work. Your job as the leader is to build your competency to see the clouds and address them. It is equally important to develop the capacity of the team to self-manage their clouds and be comfortable naming them when they show up in their teammates. A standard rule – if you go through any step in the Honest Culture Journey and no clouds are visible, then truth is not being spoken or heard.

Big Ideas from Chapter 1

Let me summarize this and put some context around it: change is hard and there will be pain when we learn the hard way.

Here is a reminder of your MUST PACK list for this journey:

- Item #1: Clarity on your beliefs about leadership, people, and relationships

- Item #2: A clear and objective view of yourself

- Item #3: Trust established to x%

- Item #4: Clear relationship context

You can go on the journey without one of these items, but it would be like camping without matches, driving across the country without a cell phone, or going to college with no money for anything besides school, books, and food. You can do it, but it will just make it harder and could put the whole journey at risk. I have travelled this Honest Culture Journey loop thousands of times as a worker, leader, entrepreneur, husband, brother, brother-in-law, son, son-in-law, father, and friend. So know that behind everything I share is experience and perspective based on real experiences that have generated great joy and great pain. I only write about things I have felt.

We will focus our work on the boss to employee and peer to peer relationships as they progress through the Honest Culture Journey. I know the things you will learn to build stronger relationships, increase the performance of your team, and create a culture that results in these two objectives being met over and over again will impact these two relationships. Are you ready? Let's start a journey together.

Chapter 2

Clear Targets

Strategy without tactics is the slowest route to victory.
Tactics before strategy is the noise before defeat.
Sun Tzu

Sometime after I got married, I became a runner. The main reason is because I had a friend who liked to run 5K races and I found it to be a cheap and easy way to stay in shape. Then I met another friend who liked to run a little bit longer, and before I knew it, I was training for a 25K race (15.5 miles).

Over the next fifteen years, I completed 25+ races of 12 miles or more, including 6 marathons, 1 ultra-marathon (32 miles), and 13 25K races. I never really considered myself a runner; if I was in shape for a race, I was generally able to rank in the top 50% for my age group, so I was not really that fast. One of the main reasons I was able to complete this was simple: I had a series of goals for myself and, with some friends, we worked to complete them.

> *Dreams without goals are just dreams.*
>
> *Denzel Washington*
>
> **99**

In one of my ebooks for leaders, *Don't Avoid the Gaps,* I make the case that it is a critical part of the leader's job to create a gap for the organization as a way of challenging a team to achieve a higher level of performance. In my running story above, having a goal for a longer race gave me a reason to run longer distances and try other things like track work and cross training to help me achieve my goal. Without the challenge of a target, I would have simply kept doing what I normally did – running 2 to 3 miles a couple of times each week.

Remember leaders: the tension created by targets that stretch your teams can make your organization stronger and healthier because of all the positive outcomes that happen when work goes into achieving a goal. Here are a few:

1. Your leadership team works together to create a plan for achieving the goal.

2. You commit to a goal that your team needs from you and complete it. Trust starts to build because you are demonstrating to them your focus on following through on commitments.

3. Your leadership team builds their capacity to overcome the issues that threaten the completion of the plan.

4. Conflict between teams arises when resources get scarce and they have to work together.

5. Striving causes mistakes to happen because no plan or performance is perfect. We learn from failure, so the opportunities to learn will increase when we strive and leaders will be challenged to put their egos aside for the greater good of the organization.

6. Leaders who do not have the capacity to grow will be singled out because they want to maintain the status quo – which has been holding back the performance of the organization for years. It's just easier to see now.

You might look at numbers 5 and 6 above and wonder how they could be positive outcomes?

Reaching targets requires learning. The reality is mistakes will happen. Those who don't want to strive will work hard to cover up mistakes or avoid situations where they might fail by fighting to take the safe or traditional path. It will take great courage on your part to confront this head on – to help the team move past these challenges or to make changes to your team.

It all starts with targets, so let's learn how to set them.

What does setting a target look like?
The beginning of any journey starts with answering two questions:

- Where are we going?

- How will we know when we have successfully arrived?

For a leadership team, you might call it setting a business plan or creating a budget. In EOS, we capture the strategy in a Vision/Traction Organizer™ which is a one-page summary of the vision for the organization along with the key goals and rocks for the next year. For a job, it could be the key duties or metrics you are trying to complete. If it's Monday and you are looking toward Friday, it could be a post-it with 5 to 7 things you need to complete. If it's 8am and your phone is flashing with an unthinkable number of messages, having that light dimmed by 5pm is the target.

> *If you don't know where you are going, you will wind up somewhere else.*
>
> *Yogi Berra*

99

You could sign up for an MBA or scour the Harvard Business Review to get some very effective teaching on creating plans for you or your organization. At the end of this book, I have a list of great resources to continue your learning. However, I have two key requirements for target setting that must be part of your process:

1. It must be a conversation, not a presentation.
My definition of a conversation is simple: an event where two people share what they truly think and feel, and both leave feeling heard and aligned on what happens next.

I have seen very few Conversations start with a PowerPoint slide deck. There is something permanent about creating a presentation, especially when it is nicely done. We all know that hours of work went into it, so it seems like a final draft. Feel free to start with a whiteboard, but don't make the presentation before the conversation happens.

I was asked by a leader to help them implement EOS in their business. As part of the process, we take two days to complete the vision for the organization using a process where the leadership team answers eight questions together. The leader called me in a panic before the first day we were going to spend together because he had not completed the vision to bring to the team. He thought it was his job to complete the vision, and this was after I had openly shared at least three times that the process we were going to use involved everyone on the team.

Some leaders are hard-wired that vision must come from them, and the result is either a plan that does not receive team support or a plan that never gets written down and shared. This was the condition of the organization when I started working with them, and the team had a bitter taste in their mouth because the vision had always been handed down to them from the CEO and the board. It took almost three months of working together before the team believed they were partners in the process and the CEO finally stepped back and welcomed the input from the team.

2. Start with the questions you need the team to struggle with.
In my book, *People-Centered Performance,* I state that one of my core beliefs is *all great conversations start with a question.*

The key question that has to be answered for this step is: *What are we trying to achieve?*

The question is pretty simple. Yet when we ask it and listen to the answers or reactions of the other people involved in the conversation, it will uncover all sorts of critical information we need for this journey.

Things like:

- Alignment and support for a common goal

- Differing opinions on the target

- Key input on what it will take to accomplish the goal

- Fear of the change and what it will mean to the team or someone's job

- Open resistance to any change

We accomplish this step by having a conversation, answering the key question, generating new critical questions, and really listening to the other people we invite to this conversation.

Visualization is important. In my thousands of hours working with teams, I see this mistake made too often – we talk and decide without any visualization of the plan for the team to see. Whether it's a large whiteboard, a document on a large monitor, or a shared document on a common drive, this step must happen visually.

Never tell someone something you can show them.

Floyd Wickman

There are additional benefits you'll receive by doing this that will make your job as a leader easier. If you design the process correctly, when the target is set the only extra work to do will be to create the specific steps in the plan to complete it. The second critical benefit is that the process creates alignment and obtains the all-important 'buy-in' from your team. Arguments help make opinions heard, with the understanding that when we leave the room with a decision, we all support it. Think how much easier your job becomes as a leader if you can have your whole team rowing together with the same cadence and in the same direction?

I will share with you a simple method you can use to create Clear Targets with your team. Before I do that, I would like to share some wisdom from experienced and successful leaders:

 Truth ——————— *Insights in Leadership* ———————

Paul Doyle

Planning isn't just a list of ideas. It's an aligned and coordinated list of ideas whose purpose is to achieve a higher goal. If you can't get the coordination, you can't get the alignment. Then it's nothing more than everybody kind of putting their activities or to-do lists in front of each other – and that's not planning.

Truth *Insights in Leadership*

Rick Baker

Micromanaging is when the leader has to know every detail, and people just do what the manager tells them. It limits the capacity and the creativity of the team because they're just waiting for someone to tell them what to do.

Here's a simple format to direct and document the conversation. (Note that we begin with the end in mind, so we define the goal first then move to the current state.)

Question 2: What is the current state?	Question 3: What are the key steps we need to complete to achieve this target?	Question 1: What are we trying to achieve?

Question 4: What are the key questions that must be answered for us to increase our certainty to 90% that we will successfully achieve this goal? (Tip: This challenges the hallway talk to come into the session room and will drive open and honest dialogue.)

Let me clarify the numbering of these questions, because this is the order in which they need to be answered.

Tips for effectively answering Question 1:
What are we trying to achieve?

Question 1 is all about dreaming of a desired future state by creating the target. Somebody starts, and the conversation that ensues involves discussing and debating it until either consensus is reached or the leader in the conversation breaks the tie and makes the decision. Dreaming is healthy and energizing.

A critical point to make is that the goal of this step is not to quiet the voice of the skeptic, but to openly invite it. I have been on several teams that have nicknamed a person 'Eeyore' after the *Winnie the Pooh* character who was always a pessimist. You will need your Eeyores for effectively answering Question 4. If you are the Eeyore in the team, your challenge is to fully participate in this step without bogging it down with what you call realism and others call pessimism.

Truth — *Insights in Leadership* —

Rick Baker

In my experience, I see people start with the *what* too often and too soon. So you're trying to explain to the person what they need to do, and they never understand the *why*. If they don't ever understand *why*, then it's hard for them to build their own passion for it. I think passion is important. Passionately Pursue Excellence is one of our key values at the Grand Rapids Chamber. I believe people bring more of themselves and more of their creative thinking when they're passionate about the work. That passion comes from the why.

Truth ——— *Insights in Leadership* ———

Dr. Donna Lowry

I learned early on that when there's not a good grounding in the why, work will be less successful. This was a lesson that was really ingrained in my leadership toolbox through my role as a parent. This skill transfers to medical education, because in some ways you're kind of parenting as a leader in medicine. When things are unexpected, commonly people feel out of control. If they don't know the reason behind something, fear may get in the way of their ability to do the right thing.

Tips for effectively answering Question 2:
What is the current state?

Question 2 is all about facing the current reality and naming it. As problems get bigger and bigger, this is a critical step because it allows the team to confront the brutal facts. Jim Collins talked about this in his book *Good to Great*, in what he called the Stockdale paradox.

You must never confuse faith that you will prevail in the end – which you can never afford to lose – with the discipline to confront the most brutal facts of your current reality, whatever they might be.

Admiral James Stockdale

99

This is also where data becomes important – so we can settle on the objective criteria that teams can cling to on this journey.

Remember:

> *Fear and fearlessness all result in the same destructive behavior: emotion-based decision-making. Not everything can be easily measured, but it's important in this step to push the team to either point to the data or go create it.*
>
> Scott Patchin

99

This step will be more difficult if some of the key processes in your business are not defined. In EOS, we coach clients to document their core processes, then spend lots of time getting all these processes to a state of what we call 'followed-by-all' or FBA. A crucial component of FBA is putting measurables in place so that the efficiency and effectiveness of the process can be constantly and consistently seen. If you lack measures for something you are trying to achieve, you need to create them.

Truth   *Insights in Leadership*

Rick Baker

What advice would you give a leader starting a new job and being asked to come up with a plan?

In every community I've moved to, I haven't come in with, "Here's the plan," right away. My first step is to get to know the community first. My priority is to spend time listening and understanding, because every community is unique. That involves listening to the business owners, listening to the staff, listening to the board. Asking questions like:

- What's going on in that community?

- What's the sticking point in the local business community?

- What's the opportunity for us as an organization to be able to solve that problem?

- What's the void in the community that we can fill?

I think a lot of it is beginning the planning process. It's a lot of listening.

 Truth — *Insights in Leadership* —

Javier Olvera

When we became entrepreneurs, we had a plan. It was not written down, but it was clear to all of us: expand our grocery stores to 20 stores within 10 to 15 years. It drove us to start really fast. From that first business in 2006, we launched a second store in 2010 and a third one in 2011. But that initial plan did not have some of the financial detail behind it to help us track our progress and make cash and debt decisions. Luckily, our banker/partner brought that up and educated us on some foundational items for healthy growth. Adding that financial piece to the plan and staying focused on it has put us in a position for the next phase of growth. In our case, that includes acquiring real estate around one of our stores so that we can expand from just being in the grocery business to also being a real estate developer in the communities we serve. It is a different business, but it aligns with another key part of our plan, our passion. Our passion is to build up and serve the Hispanic community in West Michigan.

Tips for effectively answering Question 3:
What are the key steps we need to complete to achieve this target?

This is the easiest step if the Conversations around the first two questions were open and honest. Most leadership teams are full of people who are skilled at seeing the work that needs to be done, so answering this question is all about naming the work, defining the deadline things need to be completed by, and deciding on the person who will make sure it gets completed.

Here are two things to watch for that could threaten this step:

1. Too much detail:

There will be people who want to identify a high level of detail in this step so that the project becomes 20 to 100 items. Resist this and instead focus the leadership team's energy on the outcomes we are trying to achieve and the deadlines. If a leader needs more detail, it is their to-do to sit down with some of the people actually doing the work (who are not in the room) and have them come up with the detailed plan.

2. Unclear outcome:

The thing I see most often with teams is not pausing long enough to get clarity on the outcomes that need to be achieved along the journey. If some of the targets are 12+ months in the future, it is critical to have intermediate goals. In EOS®, we add intermediate plans for the next 90 days and ask the team to make all their detailed plans with 90 days as their target timeframe. To help the teams create a clear outcome, I ask them to complete this sentence: In 90 days, to achieve the goal or make progress toward achieving the goal, success is: _____ .

Finally, it's important to add specific names and deadlines to the detail around Question 3. This, coupled with a focus on making sure the team is clear on the outcomes they want, will allow accountability to exist and delegation to happen to key people who are not in the planning session. In the Honest Culture Journey, the target is usually a team goal. It's something that will take cooperation and teamwork from multiple people. This allows for building of organizational trust.

Truth — *Insights in Leadership*

Diana J. Wong, PhD

I am a planner, so I already have a framework in my head. When I plan, a critical first step is about gathering the input because it's really important that people commit themselves. The way to have people commit themselves is that they come up with the answers first. As an example, if I say, "Okay, here's the plan, Scott. This is what we're going to be doing," that is actually a demotivator. I approach it by saying, "Okay, let's hear what everyone has to say," and then in my head I have a grid or a framework already. As I gather input from the team, I am mentally thinking, okay, that's been checked. That's been checked. That's really good.

In my experience with many teams, what happens on a team is not everyone will get all of the framework, but they will add to part of a framework and fill in most of the pieces. My role as a leader is to hold that framework and hold that space.

> *Hold the Space (definition):* Being able to allow time and presence to really listen and hear what people have to say, and then integrating and connecting it with other ideas that have been shared and put on the table. When done well, it ensures that whatever input is shared finds a place while people are in the space.
>
> The key to the process is designing it to get input and

> appreciate the ideas from other people. The outcome
> is to increase their ownership of and motivation toward
> the success of the plan. A term I use to describe getting
> the team involved in the process is co-creative. Once
> I have a plan in place, there's flexibility in altering it.

Tips for effectively answering Question 4:
What are the key questions that must be answered for us to
increase our certainty to ~90%+ that we will successfully
achieve this goal?
Let me reinforce the importance of this step by reminding you of two
critical outcomes for the Honest Culture Journey and the speaking
and hearing of truth:

1. First, it is a foundational honest conversation to proactively
   address the risks of the project by airing all the risks, fears,
   possibilities, and even innovative thinking from the team.
   This increases the chance that the best plan is put into place.

2. Second, it helps you build a healthy and smart team – and to
   test it. Debate informs and educates everyone through hearing
   different opinions. Speaking and hearing truth is healthy for the
   team. It will also make unhealthy relationships and behaviors
   more obvious because they cannot hide when open and honest
   conversation is required.

An easy way to achieve a high level of certainty in Question
4 is to use the 6 Thinking Hats® exercise by the DeBono Group
(*Debonogroup.com*) It will help surface fears, reservations, dislikes,
excitement, additional data needed, alternatives, and new ideas. If
done effectively, the risk of a hallway conversation should greatly
decrease. Here is a brief overview of how it works:

- Conversation 1 (White Hat Thinking): What information is known or needed about our goal or current state?

- Conversation 2 (Yellow Hat Thinking): What would be the positive value or benefits from achieving the outcome?

- Conversation 3 (Black Hat Thinking): Be a devil's advocate and explore why it might not work. What might go wrong? What are the difficulties or dangers?

- Conversation 4 (Red Hat Thinking): What feelings or emotions (both positive and negative) are generated in you when you look at the goal and current state?

- Conversation 5 (Green Hat Thinking): Think creatively – what possibilities, new ideas, or alternatives do you see as you think about what we are trying to achieve?

 Insights in Leadership

Jane Clark

Note from Scott: I included this bit of wisdom because it was so obvious, and yet too many of us miss the opportunity to practice our plan. When the stakes are high, and just sitting and thinking about it will likely increase the size of the clouds, please consider the words from Jane.

The other tool we use to help with feedback is a real commitment to practicing. We do dress rehearsals of everything here. That way if you plan it well, it goes well. That includes dress rehearsals for your big events, that one- on-one, or that really important conversation. Here's an example. Before we have a board meeting, we step aside during the staff meeting beforehand to practice going through the agenda. If any staff person has a speaking part in that board meeting, we'll practice what they're going to say.

Another example of our habit of practicing is around events. When we have a member event, in order to create a great experience, we will have the whole staff start outside of the venue and say, "Okay, we'll pretend we're our members when we go inside the building. What's the experience going to be? How are you going to be greeted? Where are you going to go? Where are the coat racks?" Another example is if we have a tough conversation scheduled with a partner, the people doing the conversation practice it, and we act as the partner. We give feedback and sometimes do another rehearsal until they are prepared for the conversation.

Insights in Leadership

Dr. Donna Lowry

Moving a planning conversation toward a place where you feel it has the best opportunity for success requires a leader to listen. My advice to a new leader is simple: Ask, don't tell. Also, ask often. Here are some questions I find myself repeating often:

    1. What do you think?

    2. If this variable is added, how would you think differently in this situation?

The second question sets up the opportunity to do some real-time scenario planning when dealing with a question or issue. It is a skill I used often in my medical leadership roles, and I have found it to be a very effective listening technique in my current role.

Tip: In order to avoid paralysis by analysis, if the uncertainty of the outcome is high, make sure to do rigorous planning and put a review rhythm in place that is frequent enough for the leadership team to adjust the plan as the learning happens through the execution of the work.

A theme I repeat often is: *it is that simple, and not that easy.* Plans are always perfect and conditions never change in a place we call Utopia, and that is not the world we live in.

Managing the clouds
For the Clear Targets step, here are some specific actions you can take or behaviors to watch for that will make seeing clouds easier.

As a general rule for seeing all the clouds, always create targets with all of your team involved in the activity.

 Ego:
1. Facilitate an open discussion on current states where all performance gaps are discussed and agreed upon. Too much will ignore gaps, often assuming effort will overcome anything. Too little will be silent.

2. Facilitate open discussion on *What has to happen to achieve this target?* Agree on specific dates. Same comments on ego above.

 Fear:
1. Open discussions on answering three facilitated questions mentioned in ego. Fear will show up differently than ego because there will be more emotion attached to it. If you see fight-or-flight behavior, that points toward the presence of fear.

2. Facilitate the documenting questions that still need to be answered. The DeBono 6 Thinking Hats method will help this. Fear will tend to show up when people can only effectively wear the black hat and are quiet when white, yellow, green, or red hat Conversations are happening.

Self-doubt:

Facilitate or make the assignment to complete specific plans to achieve any targets that are set. Self-doubt will show up most often as the inability to create a plan or creating one that is too slow or safe and misses the agreed-upon target in timing or delivery.

 Insights in Leadership

Paul Doyle

I think anybody who winds up in a leadership role – particularly for the first time in a kind of a senior role – who tells you that they don't have any self-doubt... I'd worry about that person. There's nothing that prepares you well for the senior role, and so you better have self-doubt. That self-doubt better motivate you to do two things: work your ass off and be open to influence. It's the point where self-doubt needs to turn over to "I need the help of the team. I do have weaknesses. I do have shortcomings, but we're better together." Self-doubt is still true in me, and it's not like I'm running around feeling insecure. But when you run into a really complex situation, and you sit, and you do all the thinking that you possibly can... you still wonder, "Geez. Have I done enough? Have I thought enough? Have I considered all the possible angles? Is there something I'm missing?" It's at that point I have to take my own advice and bounce it off someone else to see if I missed something. Better together applies to me too.

Crisis Thinking:
In all the discussions above, look for fight-or-flight reactions. Excessive fear tends to manifest itself in crisis thinking.

Big Ideas from Chapter 2

What strikes me about this step is the energy that gets created in a team when they see a Clear Target and feel the alignment of others around a goal. There is always a certain amount of uncertainty, fear, and self-doubt, so never make it a goal to remove all traces of clouds.

Let me take you back to the key actions that comprise the center of this model: Speaking Truth and Hearing Truth. Your test is to listen for evidence of clouds and acknowledge them by capturing them in unanswered questions, incorporating them into your definition of success, or just simply saying, "I hear you, and we need to move forward." In my experience, a majority of cloud management happens in the Conversations and Pause steps.

As we talk through the next steps, there will be plenty of time to revisit our progress and keep actively battling the clouds so that we continue moving forward on this journey.

If we all understand the plan and are committed to working to achieve it, fear loses its power.

Javier Olvera

99

Chapter 3
Conversations

People will forget what you said,
people will forget what you did,
but people will never forget how
you made them feel.

Maya Angelou

I believe that *great conversations start with a question* and *honest conversations are the foundation of great relationships.* My definition of an honest conversation is this:

1. **Equal parts** listening and talking

2. **Valuable information** for each person which they did not have before the conversation

3. At least one **shared outcome** is created

An event where two people are given an equal opportunity to listen and talk, they leave with valuable information they did not have before the conversation, and at least one shared outcome is created.

Consider these myth and fact pairings:

Myth: I like lots of voices and information coming at me. I can process more information than most people.

> Our brains are capable of speaking 112 words a minute and processing 400 words a minute. The result is that we allow our brain to fill up with hundreds of words in addition to those that we hear, assembling thoughts other than those spoken to us. To phrase it another way, we can listen and still have some spare time for thinking. Have you ever been in a conversation with someone while thinking about lots of

other things? I call this our internal voice, and it is one of the biggest distractions to our ability to listen.

I encourage you to read this article published in the Harvard Business Review in 1957. *(https://hbr.org/1957/09/listening-to-people)* It is based on some research by Ralph Nichols and Leonard Stevens and will give you a great perspective on how listening has been a challenge to business leaders for decades. It will also share some simple solutions that are as timeless as the problem.

Myth: We are effective multi-taskers.

Fact: Research at Stanford University has shown that we are not effective at multi-tasking. The basic research was to test our memory when we are multi-tasking – a situation many of us find ourselves in when we are doing work, having email alerts go off on our computer, having texts come in on our phone, and being interrupted by people around us. The results showed a poor performance on cognitive memory tasks. In summarizing the research, Anthony Wagner makes the point that, "There's not a single published paper that shows a significant positive relationship between working memory capacity and multi-tasking."
(Stanford News, 10/25/2018)

Myth: Facebook and other social media tools are a leading contributor to the trend of decreasing the occurrence of depression and increasing the success of marriages.

Fact: I have never seen a study enforcing this, but let me put my futurist hat on and predict this. Does anyone honestly believe the headline *Social Media Improves Our Mental Health* will ever appear in the New York Times? In her book,

Alone Together: Why We Expect More from Technology and Less from Each Other, Sherry Turkle makes the point that "Technology is seductive when what it offers meets our human vulnerabilities. And as it turns out, we are very vulnerable indeed. We are lonely but fearful of intimacy. Digital connections and the sociable robot may offer the illusion of companionship without the demands of friendship. Our networked life allows us to hide from each other, even as we are tethered to each other. We'd rather text than talk."

Do any of these myths feel like facts to you? Consider this coaching situation:.

We reviewed his feedback from his team, and the message was very clear. They felt he did not value and respect their opinions. In their words, "He does not care about us as people and just tells us what to do." It was crushing feedback for a leader who really did care about his people. His assignment was to spend a week observing his behavior with his team and the frequency he asked people's opinions versus telling them what to do. At our next meeting, he shared this realization: when he was in his office having one-on-one conversations, he asked questions and felt himself really listening. But when he was walking through the operations, which was 95% of his day, and he met up with people who asked him a question or shared a frustration, he almost always answered by telling them something to do. In that situation he felt more hurried and distracted, and rarely, if ever, asked questions.

The foundation of an honest culture is honest Conversations where people speak and hear truth. We are wired to process more words than can be spoken to us. Think of your own habits with the data and messages that flow through just your phone alone every day. All of this information, coupled with changes with customers, our people, and the general noise that happens during a day, causes our Clear Targets to lose clarity. To fight this, leaders must learn to master the Conversations that happen so clarity is preserved and the reality of our environment is reflected in our plans.

The critical interactions we need to master
I think of a guy I pass every year or so – I say, "Hi Troy," and he always responds with "Hey Superstar!" I realized years ago that he doesn't know my name, but he's a nice guy and I don't hold it against him. It's just an interaction.

Not every interaction needs to become a conversation. As a leader, you must develop a sense of when you need to slow down or create time to really listen. As we go through this section, I'll share with you wisdom from other leaders who have developed this skill and have built a reputation for effectively using it.

Here are the critical interactions you need to master as a leader:

- Walking past each other in the office

- Short meeting / Stand-up

- Email / Text

- Phone call

The Honest Culture definition of a Conversation

Before we review each of these Conversations, let me share three things that have to happen to make it a true conversation:

1. **Equal parts** listening and talking

2. **Valuable information** for each person which they did not have before the conversation

3. At least one **shared outcome** is created

A tip to remember this is the acronym EVS. Let this become your measure of a true conversation.

Remember: not every interaction is a conversation. Here is the bar I will set for you: a brief hello, a handshake, a hug, or even a brief chat about weekends happens to all of us and impacts how we feel on any given day. However, these are not Conversations because they don't create connections that build relationships.

Here's how to use these three pieces to define what makes a conversation:

1. **Equal parts listening and talking:** If we interact for a minute, do we each get a chance to ask questions AND answer questions – and are both of us really listening?

2. **Valuable information for each person which they did not have before the conversation:** I am concerned by leaders that say, "I hate small talk," because they basically avoid any conversation not related to work or do it with the attitude that 'I have to do this' – and it shows. If you are that person, remember there are lots of people (like me) that place value on getting to know

teammates. 'Valuable' is a subjective measure that will differ by individual, and yet when we are able to meet that threshold for all it makes the conversation very powerful.

3. **At least one shared outcome is created:** Time is precious, so imagine if we could leave each interaction with some shared outcome? Think of the value of these outcomes:

   • Shared feeling that this person cares about me

   • Common feeling of comfort and trust because we can be vulnerable with each other

   • Common direction on a key priority for the day/week

   • Shared understanding of a key problem which we can meet later to discuss and solve

   • Shared confidence that one of the two of you is on track to solve an important problem

   • Shared confidence that something is getting done

   • Agreement to disagree – and meet later to figure it out if needed

An interesting experiment would be to track all your interactions today and see how many can be considered Conversations? I bet you would be shocked at how few real Conversations you actually have.

Armed with my definition of a true conversation, let's take a deeper dive into each critical conversation type to develop a common understanding of how we can use these, as leaders, to develop an honest culture within our teams.

Interaction #1: Walking past each other in the office

We have lots of these. For those that work remotely, you miss this and have to use other means to create these casual encounters and turn some of them into Conversations. Let me point out that it's not important to make all these meetings true Conversations. Imagine walking between meetings, passing 10 to 20 people, and trying to make each a one-minute interaction? That's not possible. However, if we just stay alert, walking by people reinforces simple information like: they are at work, they lost weight, they have a new hairstyle, or I don't recognize this person. Make a practice to stop every now and then to share a perception or be curious about them and ask a simple question. Sometimes the person asks a question back, and sometimes you agree to connect later when you both have time to take a deeper dive into a topic that comes up (shared outcome).

Be careful of discounting this as 'just' small talk, because you will miss opportunities to create some great Conversations.

Truth — *Insights in Leadership* —

Paul Doyle

On getting feedback beyond your team: It is really important. I learned a long time ago that I will never respond to or commit to anybody other than my direct reports. So if I'm out on the floor, in a sales meeting, or anywhere else, if there's something I think should have happened, I listen to the comments, then the leader and I will talk about that afterwards. I will never act as their leader, because if I do, I've just created weakness in the structure. I've enabled people to go around, and I haven't given the leader a chance to perform.

My typical response sounds something like this, "I hear what you're saying. Have you talked with your leaders about this? I'm not going to solve this problem for you, I will make sure this gets to the right people to solve." Every engagement I have below my direct reports is exclusively listening or coaching, but never a deciding thing.

Insights in Leadership

Javier Olvera

When people are telling me something, I work very hard to pay attention to what they say and how they say it. I really look for the meaning of what they're trying to say. A common thing that I have learned to do is to initially say, "I hear what you're saying. Keep going."

Because I am an owner, many people will start conversations being very timid with me. Once they open up, that's when I start asking more questions about the topic. As an owner, one of my lessons learned is to listen, but not jump to a commitment to fix it right there. We have a team of front-line leaders who are in charge of the day-to-day work in our business. I made that mistake a few times and finally we came together as a leadership team and made the commitment to take issues we hear to the manager in charge.

Interaction #2: Short meeting / Stand-up*

*Note: A stand-up is simply a short meeting where nobody sits. It's designed for a group to update on key information, solve some problems quickly, and identify any other problems that need to be solved that day for the greater good of the team and/or organization. It is a common term in manufacturing organizations and goes by other names in different industries – for example, in healthcare it's called rounding.

In the most recent COVID-19 crisis, I've been impressed with the number of my clients who knew instinctively to start daily meetings in order to review progress on solving key problems, identify and solve other problems, and make sure everyone was getting what they needed to have a productive day.

I'll review the Pause step in the next chapter, but let me differentiate the Pause from the Conversation. Here are the key elements of a true Pause:

• Brings multiple people together

• Designed to be a more in-depth review of a target, a problem-solving session, or a review of the last 7 to 28 days of performance

• Occurs in a space where people can block out distractions

In contrast, a conversation is:

• An impromptu or unstructured interaction

• Designed to help a leader get a basic understanding of:
  • I know what's on someone's mind
  • I know what help they need from me
  • I can trust them because they are accomplishing what they committed to

For effective stand-ups, the shared outcomes for everyone involved are: clarity on who is doing what, transparency on who needs help plus a plan to address it, and increased trust among the team. The unspoken shared outcome is feeling supported and cared for. There is no magic in these meetings, just a basic agenda that creates a basic expectation on what needs to be shared or discussed.

——————   *Insights in Leadership*   ——————

Rich Sheridan

(Joy, Inc.: How We Built a Workplace People Love)

At Menlo Innovations, a company based in Ann Arbor, Michigan, they do a daily stand-up. Here is Rich Sheridan describing their tradition: In place of unproductive weekly status report meetings, we've instituted a daily stand-up ritual. Our daily stand-up occurs every day at 10am, regardless of who is in the room, and it goes the same way whether James and I are there or not. It almost always finishes in thirteen minutes or less, even if the group is as large as fifty or sixty people.

A dartboard alarm goes off at 10am to signal that it's time for the daily stand-up. Everyone stands up and gathers in a rough circle to report out to the group. Someone grabs a Viking helmet to start the meeting. The pair partners holding the helmet describe what they are working on and where they might need help. The helmet is passed to the next pair in the circle, all the way around. The last pair closes with "Be careful out there." This ends the daily stand-up.

Where does your organization need this meeting? Do you have any meetings like this that do not meet the criteria of a true conversation? By themselves, stand-ups might not exactly fit the conversation standard I have set, but experienced leaders use them religiously to help generate the daily Conversations that help a business and its people stay focused and on-track.

Truth — *Insights in Leadership* —

Paul Doyle

When we do our dailies, I will tell you that 70 percent of what we're talking about in there and what we report on is pretty much useless. But 30 percent is a surprise to somebody. The big comment I often hear is: "You're working on what? And why?" If we didn't have the opportunity to deal with that before it became a problem, it could have been a real big problem. I mean, things came up in there that would have caused much, much bigger problems if they got more than 24 hours old. An example of the impact it has had on us during COVID is our on-time delivery percentage. We have been doing a 15-minute stand-up in the morning and a 10-minute meeting in the afternoon, and the impact is nothing slips through the cracks. We have a trailing 12-month record right now of 99.99% on-time delivery. We haven't missed anything! Even with shortened staff or equipment outages that happen from time to time. I am really proud of the team.

Interaction #3: Email / Text

I put these two together because they are both 100% electronic and have to be interpreted through words and assumptions by receivers. As a result, they both present the same challenges in meeting our three criteria of true Conversations:

1. Equal parts listening and talking

2. Valuable information for each person which they did not have before the conversation

3. At least one shared outcome is created

As with passing someone in the hallway, not every email or text interaction needs to be a conversation. Yet, can you look back on all your text and email strings from yesterday and identify some that should have met this definition and did not? You are not alone if you say yes. Based on all the coaching Conversations I have had, this is a common issue that all leaders need to figure out or it will create extra drama and/or work for them that makes their job harder.

Here is one story to illustrate this:

At one point in my career, I received a complaint about a particular salesperson who was creating conflict because most of his emails were sent out with 75% of the words in all capital letters. Many people on the team felt like he was yelling at them. To use a more current term, they felt bullied. I sat down with him and shared the feedback, and to my surprise he was shocked. (I was surprised because my perception of him was that he was kind of a jerk.) He shared with me that he used caps so it was clear what the key information was and in cases where he was passionate or excited about certain things. In his eyes, it was to share emotion and not a sign of the volume of his voice.

Here are a few guidelines on how to have true Conversations through email/text/IM:

1. If you want it to be a conversation, your emails/texts need to ask a question and share information (Subject example – Key information and one question)

2. Plan on a minimum of two emails/texts from each person in the string

3. Final email/text should include: 1) Shared outcome(s) clarified (i.e., decision, emotion, next steps) and 2) Confirmation of agreement (thumbs up, etc.)

4. If you sense or experience a high level of emotion during the exchange, or that you are not getting the whole story, schedule a Pause or make a plan to bring it up at the next scheduled Pause (more on that in the next chapter)

Any person copied and 100% silent in an electronic conversation is considered an observer, but as soon as they respond then they become an active participant in the conversation and now must meet the same three requirements to make it a conversation. Not every interaction needs to be a conversation, but the more people that are part of it the greater the risk that the interaction will lead to diverging clarity and focus for the team. Be careful depending on this tool for effective Conversations – it is just not the most effective way of creating an honest culture.

Interaction #4: Phone call
(includes tools that add video to the voice)
As I write this, we are months into the COVID crisis in the United States. Most of my clients appreciate the assistance of video calls to help them manage their business, and yet almost all are tired of doing them. In one case, I know one leader who is on video calls 5 to 7 hours every day!

I predict that these will become more common as work-from-home opportunities increase and staying home if you are not feeling well becomes more of a norm.

Just like texts and emails, these can simply be a connection point, especially if it is just a voice mail that is left. What is different about these interactions is that they have greater potential to become a Pause because they are often in real time – especially when a call is scheduled, involves multiple people, has a set agenda, and lasts an hour or more. More on that in the next chapter.

I want to focus this chapter on the more impromptu call that has the objective to check in or have a brief conversation.

Here are five questions or statements that can help leaders make a phone call a true conversation:

1. Why did the call happen?

   • What were the desired outcomes of this call?

   • What questions do I have, or what questions do you have?

   • What kind of day or week are you having? Some highs and lows?

2. What are the follow-up actions based on our conversation?

3. Just to clarify, I am taking these facts or information away from this call (i.e. restate them). Do you believe this and is there anything else you want to add to the list so we are 100% on the same page?

4. I can't see you, so tell me how you REALLY feel about the conversation we had and the next steps we discussed?

Here is an example I experienced with a coaching client. After doing a feedback exercise with his team, the message back was that:

1. You do not listen to me.

2. The only time you call is when you need something.

3. You don't care about me as a person.

The leader was shocked, because he cared for his team and felt like he went out of his way to show that. After some self-observation around his interactions with his team, he implemented a habit to do a Monday check-in over the phone. Here is the simple structure of this call:

1. He called each leader and told them his intent was to just check-in, hear about their weekend, and review the week with them to see if there was any help he could provide.

2. He answered any questions they had and made a habit out of only bringing communication items that would help keep these leaders informed on anything that was happening at the central company (they were isolated on job sites).

3. The call always ended with restating any to-do's the leader committed to or scheduling a deeper follow-up call on any big topics that came up.

This structure allowed the leader to be flexible enough to either make it a basic check-in with his team or to become a true conversation. After 3 months of this habit, his team felt cared for and listened to, totally reversing the feedback the leader had previously received.

Remember that not all phone calls have to be Conversations – some are just for a little laughter, some connection time, and little boosts to our own or others' mental health. When they have to be more, make sure you use some of this simple script to manage them into a true conversation.

Managing the clouds

As we have learned, clouds will always exist. Because of the brevity of these interactions, it's next to impossible for the clouds to be managed unless you have a high degree of empathy or self-awareness which allows you to observe and pick up or feel things that are unsaid. To simplify this topic, here are things to watch for and questions to ask that will help build your skills.

Interaction #1: Walking past each other in the office

The key to this interaction is to be familiar enough with people so that you know their name and their baseline behaviors around eye contact, nature, and stress. This is a challenging situation because these are all non-verbals, so you have to be paying attention. All of these make it easier to see changes and more comfortable to slow things down to check in.

Clouds you are most likely to see: Fear or crisis thinking

What to look for:

- Deviation in their standard of eye contact, smile, or posture; lack of eye contact when that is normal often means something big is on their mind.

- How fast they are walking: could be late to a meeting or could be an indicator of fear or crisis thinking. Log it, and if you see them later walking at a more normal pace, it might be a good time for a check-in.

  Tip: Name what you see. If you don't see the normal you expect, just tell them and ask what's behind it.

- You have an extra big smile today – What news do you have to share?

- I don't see your outgoing, confident nature today – What's on your mind?

My story: *I was walking up some stairs at the end of a five-week period where, as an executive team, we had organized and implemented a 10% staff reduction at our organization. I met Jack in the stairs and we exchanged pleasantries. Then we shared a brief interaction I will never forget.*

Jack:	Scott, you are smiling today. .
Me:	Smiling?
Jack:	Yes, I haven't seen that from you in a while. It's nice to see.
Me:	You are very perceptive, Jack. Thanks for noticing. It has been a tough few weeks.
Jack:	Take care of yourself, Scott.
Me:	I will, Jack. I will..

It was a leadership lesson that I will never forget, both because I was reminded that it matters how I show up as a leader, and how being observant and willing to say something sends a powerful message of caring.

Interaction #2: Short meeting / Stand-up

These situations provide great opportunities to interact and observe your team. The challenge is to stay alert, because while 70% of the content is routine, the 30% that is not will provide a great foundation for starting a conversation – either right there or as a follow-up action item.

Clouds easiest to see: Fear / Crisis thinking / Too much Ego

What to listen or look for:

- People sharing information that indicates there is a problem (meaning it impacts an important measurable or it most certainly will cause a customer issue) and they either don't ask for help or try and make it sound like a smaller issue than your experience would tell you.

- They share nothing. The format should always set up an expectation that everyone has something to share so either address it then or follow up with them one-on-one.

Tip: Just like in interaction #1, name what you see and ask questions to clarify.

Interaction #3: Email / Text

This is one of the most challenging mediums to move from an interaction to a conversation. Researcher Albert Mehrabian determined communication is 55% body language, 38% tone of voice, and 7% actual words spoken. This outlines the risk of email and text, because it eliminates 55% of what we would normally use, and unless someone is extremely skilled then another 38% is also not available. What this means is that we have to work extra hard to make these Conversations. *(https://www.psychologytoday. com/us/blog/beyond-words/201109/is-nonverbal-communication- numbers-game)*

Clouds can be identified, but here are some important practices:

1. Make a habit of sending or asking for emails that get right to the point. For example: standardly include the following indicators of intent or actions in your header or the beginning of your text.

   • FYI

   • Need input

   • Need help

   • Need approval

2. First paragraph (100 to 150 words) should include all the information the person needs to know surrounding the topic, the input needed, and the deadline.

3. All feelings should be named or expressed in words: excited, thank you, confused, stuck.

4. Where possible, assign a number to your commitment: 60% convinced of this solution, 70% against the idea.

   The overall goal is to take the guesswork out of what people are feeling – the 93% we can't sense without being in person.

   By making a practice of these three standards, some of the same things we have learned about identifying the clouds of ego, fear, self-doubt, or crisis thinking can be identified. Like in every other situation, once you sense any of these it should be a trigger for you as a leader to make this interaction a conversation.

Interaction #4: Phone call
(includes tools that add video to the voice)
Clouds easiest to see: Fear / Crisis thinking / Too much ego

Here are some tips on what behaviors to look for that strongly indicate a cloud is present and how to manage it:

- **Silence:** The simplest one, just name it and invite them to share. *I am not hearing much from you today, Sue, and my goal is to end this call knowing what your priorities are, how I can help, and have a sense of what things are going on in your life today. Help me out...*

- **No questions, just answers:** By now you should see a theme; if you sense it, just name it. *Thanks for answering my question, Jim. Can we spend some time on what questions you have or things you are hearing from the team that I can help answer?*

- **Different tone than normal:** Volume, cadence, tone. As with above, when you hear it, just name it. *I am hearing something different in your voice today. Help me understand what has you excited / what is weighing you down?*

Big Ideas from Chapter 3

Conversations are some of the most challenging things to manage because they often happen in situations where there is noise that impedes our ability to listen or they require us to possess the empathy and self-awareness to pick up on subtle cues that are easy to miss.

One of the most critical behaviors for a leader is how they react when someone tells the truth. People start to learn – nothing bad happened as a result of telling my leader the truth. I didn't lose my job. In fact, I was praised. Done repeatedly, it gives them courage and ownership, and forever changes your culture.

Rick Baker

99

Truth is not a point in time. It's not one data point. Rather, it's on a continuum – not a continuum of truth, but a continuum of relationship.

Dr. Donna Lowry

99

In my own personal development, and in my experience coaching leaders, the most effective way to increase your own capacity in this area is intentional practice. I think back on the emotional reaction of the leader when his team told him, "You don't care about me." It hurt. The root cause was his inability to effectively manage the simple conversation of two people passing each other in the hall. The good news is the change is simple, just not always easy to do on your own. I encourage you to pick one interaction and practice some of the tips I have shared.

Chapter 4
Pause

*Truth-telling works best when it involves
revealing your own feelings,
not when it is used to insult others
and get your own way.*

George Leonard

I would offer the definition of a true Pause as:

An extended time together where movement stops and there is a focused and true conversation among two or more people; where relationships are deepened, transparency to all the real problems is achieved, and alignment is created.

Let me restate the three criteria of a true conversation:

1. Equal parts listening and talking

2. Valuable information for each person which they did not have before the conversation

3. At least one shared outcome is created

Let's have an honest conversation – how well do we Pause in our key relationships?
Understanding the Pause first starts with a quick look at how much time we spend together in key relationships and what we do with that time. Let's take a quick look at leadership teams and married couples – two important relationships that most of us have experienced.

Leadership teams spend, on average, about 250 hours together per year. This is the conclusion that author Michael Mankins reached in a study he conducted of top management teams, outlined in *Stop Wasting Valuable Time (Harvard*

Business Review, Sept 2004). This equates to about 5 hours per week.

A study by the Office for National Statistics found that, on average, married couples spend 2.5 hours per day together. *(Guardian, June 9, 2007).*

Let me make a personal observation: just looking at the quantity of time spent together, the state of these two relationships seems to be pretty strong. But looking at **how** the time is spent gives us a different picture, one focused on the quality of the time spent together:

1. For top management teams charged with leading an organization through a variety of strategic challenges, 85% of that time together was spent on non-strategic items. Rather than focusing on strategic issues, this time is spent dealing with operating performance reviews, the latest crisis, admin issues/policies, and workforce issues. Only about 37 hours was left for strategy development and approval. Is that enough? That is a subjective call, but as a person who helps leadership teams create and manage this through the EOS process, I would say no. In EOS we establish a baseline of 115 hours per year together focused on strategy development, review, and reset. I can assure you that once teams have this habit, the overwhelming feedback is *this is the most important time we spend together as a team.*

2. For married couples, of the 2.5 hours together: one-third (50 minutes) was spent watching TV together, 30 minutes was eating, and housework was 24 minutes. Altogether, this passive time (when little interaction is happening) eats up about 70% of the total time. The upside? We have 45 minutes of high-quality Pause time where we can be focused with a spouse – listening and really connecting.

A great Pause is difficult, and the data points to us not doing it very effectively in these two situations.

Here's an analogy I use with my EOS clients: imagine your team is cutting a path through a dense forest. They are working really hard and making great progress. As a leader, your job is to climb a tall tree and review your progress toward your goal so that the team's great work stays focused on the shortest path to the target. Without doing that frequently, the path would look like a line wandering away from the target. With that done fairly frequently, it would show corrections that keep the teams effort moving the team towards the target. Effective leadership maximizes ROE (return on effort) by helping the team find the shortest path to success.

The four parts to an effective Pause
Mastering the Pause is about being intentional and making Conversations matter. Here are the four parts to an effective Pause:

Part 1: An agenda
Before I send spouses all over the world running to their partner with an agenda in hand, let me explain. An agenda is simply a commitment to a common time and place to meet, a start and end time, some simple objectives for what will be accomplished in the time, and some structure for the conversation. Here are some examples:

Pause: Couch time for couples
Start: 9:30pm (when kids in bed) to 10:00pm
Location: Couch (a drink is optional depending on the day)

Agenda:
1. How was your day? (highs and lows)
2. Headlines – news from friends, family, kids
3. What decisions do we have to make together?

4. Looking forward, what does tomorrow / the weekend look like?
5. What else do we need to talk about?
6. End with a kiss and a hug

Pause: Leadership team weekly meeting: In EOS we call this a Level 10 Meeting™

Start: Same day / Same time / Start and end on time (90 minutes long)

Agenda:
1. Segue – Personal and professional best (5 minutes)
2. Scorecard – Review weekly numbers of the business (5 minutes)
3. Rocks – Report on status of big things that team members are working on (5 minutes)
4. People Headlines – Customer / Employee (5 minutes)
5. To Do – Review commitments from last week – Done or Not Done? (5 minutes)
6. Issues – Team problem-solving time (60 minutes)
7. Wrap-up – Review To-Do's, Cascading Messages (3 minutes)
8. Checkout – Rate meeting / Feedback on our time together (2 minutes)

An agenda is an understood flow of what will happen and when it will happen. It also sets some expectations for what all the attendees need to contribute. It is formal enough so two or more people can come together and have a true conversation. It also helps us overcome the barrier of being tired or distracted from a long day and makes it easy to engage – even if we don't really feel like it. An agenda starts slow and easy, and the harder parts or questions to answer come after the easy ones.

Part 2: Personal commitment from everyone to 90+% vulnerability, 90+% honesty, and 95%+ listening

Healthy relationships are built on the ability of the participants to be vulnerable, honest, and to authentically listen to each other. It might sound kind of hokey – but imagine starting every meeting with a shared commitment to be vulnerable, honest, and really seek to understand the other people in the room? I have never been in a Pause where this was done, but it is a critical part of an effective Pause. When I facilitate group Conversations, my job is to create an environment that is safe so this can happen and to watch for any indication that it is not happening. When I facilitate, I also make this my expectation of the group.

> **NOTE:** Why don't you put 100% here Scott?
> I have been on this earth for over 50 years and experienced lots of life events as: an observer, a close participant, and the center of the storm. These events have included: births, deaths, firings, being fired, health crisis, relationships destructing, relationships starting, relationships ending, relationships celebrating milestones, being loved, and loving others.
> In all these experiences, I have found healthy Conversations where people held back what was bothering them or that they were struggling with something because someone in the room had bigger struggles and they needed to focus on that person. I have seen this in relationships, family conversations, leadership team discussions, boss to employee, and peer to peer relationships. I don't believe 100% is possible or even healthy. Yet one of the tricks of building healthy relationships that enable this Honest Culture Journey to happen is developing the ability to choose the right 90 to 95% to share **and** being able to listen or draw out the 95% of the information you need from others around you. A good self-check for each of us as

we step into or out of an effective Pause is to rate our personal performance on vulnerability, honesty, and listening. Think too about the participants and whether you believe they were displaying an appropriate level of vulnerability and honesty?

Part 3: Clear understanding of progress to target and/or what has to change

The agenda helps take care of this, but it is worth calling out because lots of little Conversations have happened since we set our Clear Target. A Pause has to revisit that target.

- For leadership teams: This could be taking out the yearly goals every 90 days and reviewing them.

- For a married couple: This could be pulling out a financial plan every year to update it or reviewing spending/budget every month. It could also mean pulling out the family calendar and reviewing it.

The key things that are accomplished in this part are: we review the progress to a target (which is generally something positive to talk about) and discuss anything that has to change, either in our behavior or the target that we set.

Part 4: Clear action plans and list of issues not solved – yet

A great conversation creates a shared understanding of next steps. I talk a lot about how to have great meetings with leaders because in EOS we have them implement the Level 10 meeting™. One of the things leaders tell me is how much they value having clear actions leaving every meeting and how real issues get solved based on their priorities. This part is simple but having coached dozens of teams I know it is not easy. Ending every meeting by taking a few minutes to review all the next steps and owners of that work will have the biggest impact on making your Pause effective.

Truth ——— *Insights in Leadership* ———

Paul Doyle

How and what do you listen for to know that things are running well in your organization?

For me, it's the planning process. It gives me a good idea in my head of what's supposed to be happening. An analogy is the score of a symphony: when you look at it on paper, and you kind of play it in your mind, it's in the back of your head all the time. So when you're in a meeting, and you hear a *flat note,* it stands out like a sore thumb. An example is when people are saying things that I know are not consistent with the plan. That's when I raise my hand. We also meet most of the time in a meeting room where the plan is up on a big whiteboard wall, so it's always in front of me and everyone else. A plan is a great tool for listening because we all know where we are going, why we are focused on certain areas, and what the priorities should be in every department. I also hear when people are frustrated. You can see when they're running into the barriers that are preventing them from being successful through the tone that they report or the things that they report in their one-on-ones. Then I have to act. When the plan is incomplete, when people are getting frustrated, when they can't get over their own hurdles, or they need somebody to do it – you can hear it. You can see it.

Insights in Leadership

Dr. Donna Lowry

How and what do you listen for to know that things are running well in your organization?

I mean, things just get done. I know that sounds too simple, but when I see the enthusiasm people have and the joy that they're taking in the work, it provides me a great metric. When things are getting done, it's a different kind of energy. I see and hear things like "Hey, we got this done!" or actual high fives between teammates. We're a small organization, so we refer to our rock sheets and our scorecard, and when we see things get behind, which they do because we are a team that strives and sets challenging targets, we react and create plans to get things back on track. All those Conversations require honesty and expose partial honesty, and that helps me listen.

Pause mastery for leaders

We covered the four parts to an effective Pause; the next step is to master the following types of Pauses. By mastering, I mean these three things:

- Most effective frequency

- Most effective duration

- Optimizing individual and collective vulnerability, honesty, and listening

Here are some tips to start mastering these on your journey:

1. Team meeting:

a. Create a great agenda:
I already shared the agenda for a Level 10 Meeting™. [If you want to download a copy of this tool or learn more about EOS, please see the appendix.] When designing your meeting, here are the key things to include:

• Review the data

• Share headlines (aka: what are the big things on people's minds?)

• Report on progress to big things that need to be done (individual accountability)

• Solve problems for half to two-thirds of the meeting

• Always end with a review of commitments and cascading messages to others

b. Always start and end on time:
No explanation needed.

c. Choose the right frequency for recurring meetings:
The right mix of weekly, monthly, quarterly, and annual. Some leadership teams do a daily, but that tends to only be effective for operations leadership teams, frontline teams, or for a team during a crisis (2008/2009 recession, 2020 COVID-19 Crisis).

d. Insist on and coach individuals to healthy and effective behaviors:
Commitment and demonstrated ability of all participants to display appropriate levels of vulnerability, honesty, and listening.

2. One-on-one:
One-on-ones are defined by the name; it is you having focused time with one of your team members. The frequency is dependent on factors like how much individual coaching someone needs or how much trust you have in them to do their work without you checking in on it.

Similar to team meetings, here are some tips for using one-on-ones effectively:

a. **Agenda set:**
Focused on what the employee needs

b. **Frequency:**
As often as the employee feels they need the time

- As a rule, leaders need to do these at least quarterly to review/reset goals, give performance feedback, and set/revisit   development goals

- Peers should do them as often as needed, depending on how important it is to keep their departments aligned or to continuously build/strengthen the relationship between them as leaders

3. Audio / Video Conference:
Work has changed with technology and the globalization of business. As a result, some of our Pause moments have to happen through technology. After hundreds of hours spent in both video

conferences and audio-only meetings, I lump them together because mastering both of them requires the same actions as a leader.

First, let's re-examine the similarities and differences of an effective Conversation and an effective Pause:

Effective Conversation	Effective Pause
Equal parts listening and talking (despite the brief time together)	Equal parts listening and talking (despite complexity of adding > 2 people)
At least one shared outcome is created	Shared outcomes of: • Clear/revised action plans • Clear/revised vision for the work • List of issues not yet solved
In an ideal world: Same as Pause Reality: Few leaders have the skills in empathy and self-awareness to do this.	Personal commitment from everyone to exhibit: • 90+% vulnerability • 90+% honesty • 95%+ listening *measured by behavior before, during, and after the meeting

Audio or video conferences are difficult to really assess for vulnerability, honesty, and great listening. Here are things you can do as a leader to structure an agenda that constantly invites / challenges your team to live into this expectation:

1. Script great questions in key parts of agenda that invite vulnerability and honesty:

   • What things are you celebrating?

   • What is not working?

   • What is one question or outcome you want from this team today?

2. Script questions to help people listen, i.e., when the team hears these questions, they know the team is asking them to go deeper:

   • Tell me a little more about that?

   • I am hearing something in your answer – so how do you REALLY feel about that?

   • I think I heard you say . . . is that accurate?

   • What do you **really** need from this team right now?

I would add some of these right to agenda items or the top of the agenda with the reminder: *This meeting will only be as effective as our ability to be vulnerable, open, and honest and to listen well so we truly seek to understand each other and we leave with a mostly accurate understanding of where each other are.*

> Note that in the conversation chapter, I talk about the text / chat conversation. There is no such thing as an effective text / chat Pause in my opinion. It's not because we can't be vulnerable or honest, but really listening to other people is next to impossible because of the medium. I restate my key

point that if you sense or experience a high level of emotion during the exchange or that you are not getting the whole story – schedule a Pause or make a plan to bring it up at the next scheduled Pause.

The following are not top three Pause events to master but can be extremely valuable. Do not underestimate the power of these Pause times:

1. Meal together
In EOS, we specifically call out meals as trust-building time. The only agenda is to talk and listen. In some cultures, meals are almost required in building relationships, and they become even more powerful when people use them to share their culture or the team goes somewhere where the meal is actually an experience. I strongly encourage my teams to do a meal together each quarter, and the ones that do are generally higher performing teams.

 Insights in Leadership

Diana J. Wong, PhD

I use meals as a place to connect with my team, and over lunch or dinner we check in. A check-in is a debrief time when I take the pulse of the team. I typically ask questions like:

- Did you have a good day?

- If you've had a good day, tell me about it.

- Was there anything that you learned?

- Was there anything that was out of place or that didn't go as well as you wanted it to?

I might take a deeper dive into any answer. I don't necessarily do a deeper dive when things don't go well, because I'm trusting the person to solve that problem. If that problem is still not fully resolved, then we can do a deeper dive into it. Oftentimes people do know what some of the problems are; they just need to talk it out. They've got it. So really, it's about being able to just hold a space for people to share their concerns.

2. Clarity Break™

This is a term Gino Wickman defined. Personal excellence guru Stephen Covey called it *sharpening the saw*, and I bring it up because the outcome of this time is an increased ability of us as leaders to enter a Pause and demonstrate the vulnerability, honesty, and ability to listen to others. The goal with this break is to schedule 1 to 2 hours per week when you are alone and undisturbed. Spend this time to:

- Take personal inventory of how you are doing.

- Review and reset your priorities.

- Achieve the objectives of being more refreshed, refocused, and confident.

Don't underestimate the power and value of this time. The teams I work with would all perform at a higher level if 100% of the team practiced this religiously.

Managing the clouds

I want to template cloud management, but in every step it's a little different.

I hope you see that the theme for you as a leader is to work in structure so you can look for specific behaviors that will signal to you that ego, fear, self-doubt, or crisis thinking has built to a level that will likely impact the journey.

Here are the key behaviors to watch for:

1. Silence: When debating issues or sharing highs and lows, everyone should contribute. If a voice is silent, it is generally self-doubt or crisis thinking.

2. Side Conversations: I call them sidebars. Team conversation involves everyone, so when this happens, I call it out and finish the main conversation before we invite the side conversation to be put in front of the team. This is generally evidence of an ego issue or fear.

3. Weak commitment language: Words and phrases like 'kind of' or 'if I have to' tell me that the person is just going along with the flow. The other thing I listen for is their voice making a statement sound like a question. To clarify, I just ask – was that a question or a commitment? Usually they laugh and restate it with a firmer voice.

 Truth — *Insights in Leadership* —

Diana J. Wong, PhD
I listen for certain words; I have about twenty-five on the list. Here are three: *but, should, and I think.* The word *but* deletes all of what was said before. I pay attention to whether this person says one thing, but they actually mean the other. "We should increase prices, but nobody will come at all." You're just contradicting yourself, right? There is some sabotaging. I think it's a way for somebody to

dial down what they may be unsure of.

The word *should* softens a commitment. *I should do that.* When I hear that word my response is always, "Well Ramon, are you uncertain about this next step or are you ready to commit to it?" Should do it sounds uncertain, and our goal is to get to *will do it.*

I think: In a recent conversation with a coaching client she made the statement, "I think I have a science-y mind." She is uber-scientific with knowledge. My response was, "Well, Melinda, do you think you have a science-y mind or do you know?" She goes, "I know I have a science-y mind." I say, "Claim it then." You don't have to be arrogant about it, because women often worry about that. They use this moderated language to diminish themselves.

4. Hiding opinions behind tactfulness: Statements tempered with safe language like 'I feel' or 'I wonder' helps to soften our opinions. The intent is to create a safe space for everyone's opinions. Too often, the impact I observe is that it makes it harder for teams to have conflict rather than easier. In EOS, we have a comeback phrase: "Say it in one sentence and hit the nerve," which invites people to just say it.

5. Politicking: I love sharing this observation at the beginning of a session, "If you say it once, it is your opinion; if you say it twice, you are politicking." The root of repeating is ego or crisis thinking. 'We have to do what I say, so let me repeat it'. The other is two people repeating their position repeatedly to each other. When you see two ego clouds grow, address it head on.

6. Not prepared: One meeting is not really an issue, but multiple meetings usually show crisis thinking. The person is so mired in something that the cloud comes in with them and they see nothing but what is right in front of them.

The theme here is to create an agenda so behaviors that indicate the existence of the clouds of Ego, Fear, Self-Doubt, or Crisis Thinking become obvious. The hazard of striving for an outcome is that it decreases your ability to practice empathy, which is a skill that makes it easier to see clouds. The key for all on the team is to name it and deal with it. We are also charged as individuals to know when we are personally being impacted by the clouds in our lives and have the courage to share it, either to ask for help or for a little grace as we try and get back on track.

An effective Pause allows for some of these deeper Conversations or observations that are almost impossible to consistently accomplish in a regular conversation.

 Truth ———— *Insights in Leadership* ————

Jane Clark

A concept I learned in EOS called *36 Hours of Pain* has been transformative. If a conversation has to happen, look at it as 36 hours of thinking, preparing, delivering, and managing the outcomes. For me, the anticipation of tough conversations is way harder than the actual conversation. This pushes me to deliver it quickly and not to avoid it for days, weeks, or months.

Truth ———————   *Insights in Leadership*   ———————

Javier Olvera

My wife taught me a lesson about this, and it is pretty simple. Never have a hard conversation when you are hungry, tired, or you have been drinking alcohol. While feedback should never be just about sharing things that are not working, when you do have to have that conversation, the best time is after lunch, in the early afternoon.

Big Ideas from Chapter 4

The Pause is a powerful tool for one-on-one or team effectiveness.

Working with teams navigating the recession, COVID crisis, and many other events that threaten to derail the Honest Culture Journey, I have seen the Pause habits they establish make all the difference in the performance of the company. The key is to create the Pauses in your schedule and stick to them. The next step is to refine not only the agenda, but your ability to read and react to the behaviors that signal a cloud has entered the room and is threatening the journey. The final thing is to speak the truth in the moment as successes should be celebrated, praise needs to be shared, or issues need to be voiced.

> *If you see something that has to happen, and you don't speak the truth at that moment, there's a presumption of agreement.*
>
> *Paul Doyle*

99

Of course, we are all challenged to develop as leaders so that we master our own clouds, which ironically makes our energy more available to help our teammates. It is not unlike the message we get when we enter an airplane – *Put on your oxygen mask first, then help the people around you.*

Chapter 5
Re-orient

All progress begins with
telling ourselves the truth.

Dan Sullivan

Have you ever started a diet or workout commitment in January, only to stop after a couple of weeks? You are not alone. Studies show that only 25% stay committed to these New Year's resolutions after 30 days. *(Forbes)*. Why? The simple answer is that change is hard. Just saying we are going to do something very different to what we have been doing is noble – and may be the right thing to do – but too often we are not successful in making it happen.

My intent is to be direct and hit a nerve with this next statement: saying you will do something when somewhere in your body you doubt you can do it, but not raising these concerns, is lying. Harsh? It is meant to be. How many of us would raise our hands in a room full of people if the keynote speaker asked all the people who have told lies in the last twenty-four hours to raise their hands?

Honest Cultures are built around behaviors that demonstrate speaking truth, and in turn allow us to hear truth. This is not a long step, but the key is to make sure changes are reset and agreed upon, and we are Re-oriented to any direction that the Pause established helped us define.

The critical outcomes of Re-orient are:

- Re-affirm alignment on where we are versus where we expected to be

- Document and share any new needs, including information needs for critical decisions

- Any help needed is asked for and resolved

- Work reassignments are made and communicated

The key difference from a Pause is that the Re-orient step gathers up all the key information generated by an effective Pause, provides time to document any changes, and provides time to make sure all key individuals are aligned with the decisions. If it is done effectively, we can return to Clear Targets and start the process all over again.

How to Re-orient effectively

1. Document, review, and share the Pause conversation:
First, the Pause is documented so anyone who was not there can know not only the outcome of the discussion, but also the *why* behind the decision. Here is an example of how the *why* makes all the difference:

> After a planning session, the decision was made to continue to launch a product that had a quality issue and to leave the team continuing its struggle with making the product. Telling the team to keep going with no detail risks demotivating them and creates a belief that leadership does not care about quality. By telling them the rest of the story – which is to keep making the product with the current tool because the engineering change will cost $50,000 and we need a week to talk to the customer to get their approval for the change; once we get approval, we will build some inventory, and schedule 2 days of downtime to fix the tool – helps them understand that their truth was heard. When we document and cascade messages, it helps the *why* make it to all levels of the organization. That is a key part of the Re-orient step.

2. Establish what help or resources are needed:
I used the word lying earlier. This step becomes the way we stop pretending we believe we can be successful without help. A key part of the Re-orient phase is to ensure the resources or support are aligned with the goals. An effective Pause identifies lessons learned, which will ultimately lead to revisiting the support and resources that are needed.

3. Gather any additional input:
It's possible the Pause included most of the people that needed to speak into the plan, but more often than not there is someone else that needs to provide input and feedback. An effective Re-orient step, especially one where some key changes need to be made to the plan, will pull in those voices. In this way, when we return to the Clear Targets step, the information is known.

Managing the clouds
Re-orient goes so quickly that clouds have very little impact on this step. This is because it's about communicating changes, realigning resources, and sometimes getting additional input so the Clear Targets step can happen to keep the Honest Culture Journey moving forward. The two clouds that will most likely threaten this step are ego and crisis thinking, and here is why:

 Ego:
This keeps leaders from asking for help. It is that simple, and I witness it in every team I work with. A key to making sure this does not get in the way is to never make this step the task of a single person on the team. By keeping a couple of people involved in this step, peer accountability is created and through honesty ego can be called out.

Crisis Thinking:

Not having enough time to communicate to the team is a common reason, and eventually excuse, for not informing the team on the 'why' along with the 'what' message. Just like ego, assigning someone to be accountable for the communication to the team allows the work to be divided and removes the excuse of being too busy.

Big Ideas from Chapter 5

Re-orient is a critical step because it helps build the communication and teamwork that results in a firm foundation for effective Clear Targets. By taking time to complete this step, trust is built within the broader organization and targets stay clearly defined. Skipping this step drops people from the journey because the 'why' gets lost, and the ultimate impact of that is a diminished level of energy for the target.

Chapter 6
Go lead!

*To know and to not do
is to not yet know.*
Kurt Lewin

99

Keep buggering on.
Winston Churchill

99

So there it is: four simple steps, manage those clouds, and you will find yourself in this team, department, or organization where you are wildly successful, having both the relationships and results to be the envy of other leaders. It is that simple, and yet we all know it is not that easy.

Before you put down this book and throw up your hands, let me help you with the next steps in your journey. One question I ask at the end of every coaching session is: We have talked about a lot of things in our conversation, so what actions are you committing to?

Here are some next steps.

First, pick a situation or person that you want to go on this journey with. Here are your choices:

1. A person on your team with whom you want to deepen the relationship and elevate their performance, impact, and self-confidence

2. A peer where there is interdependence in your work, either individually or through your departments

3. Your leader

4. Your team

5. A group of stakeholders with whom it would be helpful to have a clearer picture of their voice and build a stronger relationship with them

My advice is to pick one where the relationship already has a strong foundation or is trending in that direction. This will help you focus your energy on finding your voice and rhythm as a leader.

If you decide to pick a difficult relationship, just remember to be patient and find a coach or mentor to be a resource, because the work will be harder. Use some of the questions shared in the context section of chapter 2 to help you start this conversation. Although it is often assumed, here are some insights that remind us how this journey goes much smoother when we already have the right people in the right seats.

Truth   *Insights in Leadership*

Jane Clark

One of the tips I would give a new leader is to focus on building a great team. EOS equipped us with the ability to do that by guiding us in defining our values. Using those values to select the right people and put them in the right seat was transformative. It's so much easier to manage and trust people who are a perfect fit for your culture and the work you need them to do. EOS equipped us to do this very well.

Secondly, create a time or a process for creating a Clear Target with them. You will hear from our experts there are very different models of creating a Clear Target for yourself and your team. Your solution should gather the voices you need to create a Clear Target and a plan to get there. A key point here is that a Clear Target does not have to be a big plan; yet it does have to come as the result of a conversation which leads to a commitment. If you are a new leader, sometimes the first few laps of your journey will be by yourself. Yet seeing you do the right thing will win over people and, like Paul experienced, they will more actively join you on future loops.

Insights in Leadership

Paul Doyle

The single biggest way to get people to speak truth to you is to act on what they tell you, especially when it's different from what you originally thought. If they can change your mind, and they can experience that, they'll speak truth to you more.

Insights in Leadership

Jane Clark

Our integrator, Jodi Owczarski, has helped build the capacity of our team to gather and hear feedback. She has ingrained two statements in our culture: *I can't fix what I don't know is broken* and *Just tell us our baby is ugly.*

We work very hard to give people the permission to tell us the truth. So we'll say, "It's okay to tell us our baby's ugly, because we can't fix what we don't know is broken."

The third step is to listen. Particularly if it is skilled listening using some of the questions our experts shared, this is the time to practice tracking the progress toward the target and how you can help. As Javier highlighted, listening can be helped by having clear financial numbers that give you a pulse of your business. It can also involve more structured Conversations like the stand-ups Paul Doyle mentioned, where you carefully listen for the critical information that tells you if things need your attention. Diana also shared her focus on key words that help her stop and make sure a conversation to move things forward happens. Review some of the information shared by our experts and pick one to start practicing during your journey.

The fourth step is to create the Pause events so the team can revisit the targets, celebrate the progress, and deal with any key barriers or market changes that have appeared since the plan was set. As the leader, create the Pause events that align with the pace of your business and create that space where a true Pause can happen. Remember Diana's focus on holding the space and being present. I would offer that you need to be intentional about becoming an expert at both, so challenge yourself to develop your own capacity in each of those areas.

Truth   *Insights in Leadership*

Diana J. Wong, PhD

In order to check that I am receiving the whole truth of a situation, I often double-check and say, "Is that all there is?" or "Help me understand this a little bit more." It's usually a dialog of double-checking and wanting to hear whether the person is disclosing more deeply, giving me more specifics, and getting closer to the heart of the matter.

What makes this easier is just knowing the person and recognizing when they are not sharing all that they could or should. For example, one of my team members will share a lot more if he is having a good day. But when his day is rough, I have to stop and say, "Hey, tell me more about that." Then he will unload the truth with a lot more detail. I need to just pay attention and create space for him to share what he needs to share.

Finally, remember that the Re-orient is just a recognition of progress and an intentional event to clearly do any resets to the plan and communicate progress or changes to the greater organization. Keeping all the groups connected and re-establishing clarity and focus for all people on this journey is a critical, and often overlooked, step. It might look like the planning wall in Paul Doyle's conference room that is constantly updated, or, if you're a company running on EOS, it could be the To Do's that get assigned after your team leaves their Level 10 Meeting™. If you choose a meal to Pause, it could be a simple email to confirm and share any reaffirmed commitments or changes to get as close to 100% clarity and alignment as you can.

The conversations with these leaders reminded me how important it is to know yourself. Dan Sullivan calls it Unique Ability®; Parker Palmer calls it the voice of vocation. Talking to each leader brought to mind a common thread of successful leaders: they understand both their strengths and the blind spots they create. Each of my interviewees reminded me of the importance of self-awareness, and the ability to balance that with hiring the right people, trusting them to reach the targets that are created, and creating the culture where people will speak up. Remember that feedback is not always to correct behavior, but also to lift us up.

Success in the knowledge economy
comes to those who know themselves
– their strengths, their values, and how they best perform.

Peter Drucker

99

Now it is time to start your journey. I will leave with the simple phrase that I have shared thousands of times:

> *Listen . . . Lead. Repeat often!*
> *Blessings on a great journey*
>
> Scott

99

My kids told me about an author / speaker they respect named Bob Goff, and he put his phone number in all of his books and told people to call him. I loved that idea, so here is mine. If you have a question or comment about this book, I would love to spend a few minutes having a conversation. Feel free to call me: +1 616-405-1018.

A Tip for Starting Your Journey

One of the outcomes of these interviews for me was the value of having relationships with people that I can call on when I need help. I have a hard time asking for help, and yet when I do it energizes me to see the willingness of people to share of themselves. If you have a group of people that are ready to help, then reach out to them and ask for it. If you don't, then find someone who would be willing to be a sounding board, coach, or mentor and use this journey to start building that circle of people.

Here is a quick tip for those of you looking to build a relationship with another leader – just set up an hour conversation and ask them the same questions I asked the six leaders that contributed to this book. Here are the questions:

1. Tell me about your first leadership role (have people reporting to you) – how did it happen and what do you remember about the role?

2   Tell me about your first role as an executive leader where you led other leaders – how was it different from that first role?

3   Creating the target: What kind of plan did you have in the first role? And what kind of plan existed in the first executive leadership role?

4   How has planning evolved for you over the years? What does it look like today?

5   Listening: What does a typical day look like for you as a leader – from the first time you get up to when you go to bed?

6   What are the things you look / listen for to assess progress toward the target?

7   Are there any specific words or phrases that alert you there might be a problem? Any non-verbals?

8   What wisdom would you share with a new leader around listening and gathering feedback from your team?

9   Speaking and hearing truth: Based on your experience, what are some of your barriers to speaking the truth to people? Hearing the truth?

10. How do you know you when someone is telling you the truth?

11. What guidance would you give a new leader about hearing and receiving the truth from others?

12. Cloud management: [Show them the Honest Culture Journey model and explain each of the clouds.] If you think of the teams you have led, which of these clouds have had the biggest impact on the culture and performance of teams? What have you done as a leader to minimize the negative impact?

Give yourself an hour and a half, and just listen, take notes, and ask more questions. If your experience is anything like mine, you will leave energized, smarter, and more passionate about building a team that has truth at the heart of all the work. Imagine your team demonstrating a level of performance and teamwork that makes people want to interview you! The other great thing about a successful journey is that people want to join.

Appendix

Insights in Leadership

*When I was a boy and I would see scary things
in the news, my mother would say to me,
"Look for the helpers. You will always
find people who are helping."*

Fred Rogers

Let me introduce you to some of my 'helpers':

- **Paul Doyle**
  CEO of Coastal Automotive and Coastal Container

- **Rick Baker**
  President/CEO of the Grand Rapids Area Chamber of Commerce

- **Diana J. Wong, PhD**
  CEO & President of Sensei Change Associates, LLC

- **Jane Clark**
  President of the Michigan West Coast Chamber of Commerce

- **Donna LB Lowry**
  MD, President/CEO of Ready for School

- **Javier Olvera**
  President/Co-Owner, Olvera Enterprises

Paul Doyle
CEO of Coastal
Automotive and
Coastal Container

Paul Doyle is the Chief Executive Officer of Coastal Automotive and Coastal Container, based in Holland, Michigan. Prior to joining Coastal, Doyle served as President and Chief Executive Officer of GHSP Grand Haven from 2007-2014. Paul joined GHSP in 1999 as Vice President of Human Resources and in 2003 was named Vice President of Sales and Marketing. Prior to joining GHSP, he was director of organizational development at Holland, MI-based Donnelly Corporation.

In 2016, Paul founded a leadership development practice called LeaderWork, dedicated to his passionate belief that leadership development is important and the key lies in equipping leaders with something they can start practicing tomorrow. Since its founding, LeaderWork has guided over 100 leaders through a 10-month, cohort-based journey. Paul is also a graduate of the University of Notre Dame, a published author, a mentor at the Jandernoa Entrepreneurial Mentoring program, and guest lecturer at Grand Valley State University's Executive MBA program. For more information, visit the website at **www. leader-work.com**

Insights in Leadership

Why I asked Paul to share his leadership insights

I first met Paul in an interview for a job. He was CEO of a company called GHSP and was leading their training efforts. He did not hire me for that job, and ironically, Paul and I stayed in touch. When he started a leadership program called LeaderWork, he invited me to attend and consider being part of the group to launch it. Since that first meeting, I have been working with him on what I would call a 'passion project.' We have taught together through four cohorts, and in that time I have gotten to know Paul as a caring, smart, passionate, honest, humble, funny leader and person. Selfishly, I continue to work with Paul because working with him makes me smarter and strive to become a better version of myself. Being around Paul has had that kind of impact on me. I hope you have a few Pauls in your leadership journey, and if not, I am glad to be able to include his voice in this book.

The story of Paul starting his own leadership journey

I started my career as a teacher in high school. When I completed my undergrad degree, I went right to my Master's because it was offered to me for free. So when I was twenty-five years old, after having only taught in a student teaching role at Clay High School in South Bend, Indiana, I had a license to be a high school principal because of my Master's degree in Educational Administration, which made no sense at all.

After teaching for a couple of years, I was hired back to the high school that I went to in Portland, Oregon, as the Director of Guidance.

I was responsible for college admissions and career planning in the school. Well, the principal had to take an extended leave of absence, and I was the only one who had a Master's in Educational Administration and was licensed to be a school principal. So at 27, I took on my first leadership role at my high school – the high school that I graduated from eight years before. That was probably my first leadership role.

I was given no plan. What I can remember is, first of all, I was ostensibly a leader for people who had been my high school teachers eight years before. So it was weird to begin with.

I quickly realized that no one was going to look at me and say, "He's got enough experience to lead me" or "He's got enough competence in the subject matter to lead me." I had no substantial educational experience, but I had done some cool work on theories of learning. So I leaned on those principles: how learning occurs and what learning looks like. I focused on direct instruction of critical-thinking skills.

The other thing I had that I would give a lot of credit to is my athletic experience. I understood how teams worked. I understand discipline, and I understand routines from coaching and being coached. I leaned on that during those early years as a leader.

One of my first steps was to say to myself, "What I have to do is support these people. I've got to find out what they need from me as a leader, and then I've got to try to provide that." This led me to sit down with people – some of the professors and priests that had been my teachers – and say, "What do you need from me?" Their responses were things like: help me with the discipline in the classroom, help me with the kids who are a problem, keep the parents off my back, and support my professional development.

Okay, I know how to do those things, but I would not have known that if I did not go and ask them. That single activity provided me a plan for my first leadership role.

Initially, most of the requests were transactional stuff that they were looking for. Things like discipline, resources they needed, or extra time to complete things. A couple of teachers and I got into more substantive discussions about theories of teaching and learning. One request centered on questions about the S.A.T. test. Do you teach to the S.A.T. test or do you teach kids how to think? This was an area of my expertise because of an analysis I had done in grad school using something called Bloom's Taxonomy of Learning. So we did an evaluation of the test, and it helped teachers understand how to better prepare their kids for that test. Well, a couple of teachers got kind of excited about that and said, "Will you come into my classroom and analyze my teaching style relative to those things?" So I started getting invited in more and more on the basis of the things that I could help with.

That habit and the feedback helped create the plan for me for those first days as a new leader.

> *Rick Baker*
> President/CEO of the
> Grand Rapids Area
> Chamber of Commerce

Rick is President/CEO of the Grand Rapids Area Chamber of Commerce, a 2,400-member business organization that is actively engaged in developing strong diverse leaders, supporting business growth, and advocating for a business environment that fosters economic prosperity for all.

The Grand Rapids Chamber's vision is for the Grand Rapids region to be a dynamic, nationally recognized, top-of-mind community. Under Rick's leadership, the Chamber has developed a strategic focus on three key areas: being a champion for an inclusive and magnetic community, accelerating business growth through cutting-edge programming, and providing a positive business climate by aggressively advocating for business.

Rick began his career in chamber of commerce management in May of 1988. He has held executive positions with chambers in Iowa, Illinois, and Minnesota, prior to assuming his current position in April 2011. Rick's career has allowed him to fulfill his passion as a fierce advocate for business.

Rick has an education in accounting and holds a Bachelor of Science degree from Upper Iowa

Insights in Leadership

University. He is a 1995 graduate of the U.S. Chamber Institute for Organization Management at the University of Colorado. He's a past Board Member for the Association of Chamber of Commerce Executives, member of the Metro Chambers Coalition and the United States Chamber of Commerce Committee of 100.

Locally, he serves on the Boards of Directors of The Economic Club, The Right Place, Inc., Downtown Grand Rapids, Inc., Grand Valley Metro Council, Experience Grand Rapids (where he serves as Chair of the Finance Committee), The Rapid, and the West Michigan Policy Forum.

Why I asked Rick to share his leadership insights

I met Rick at an event within the first month of him starting his job leading the Grand Rapids Area Chamber of Commerce. Since that moment, most of my knowledge of Rick has been watching his organization evolve under his leadership. I had the opportunity to help them complete their EOS® Graduation over the last year, and I have just been so impressed with the team he has assembled and the impact they have had in a community and region where I live and work. Rick is also very unique in that he is both an integrator and a visionary, so when I started to think about who I would interview for this book, his named jumped to the top of my list. I have a lot of respect for Rick after seeing the impact of his leadership first hand, so part of my interest was self-serving; I wanted to get to know Rick more because I have enjoyed working with him. For those of you challenged to go into new communities and lead, Rick is a master at it, so I am thankful he was willing to contribute to the Honest Culture Journey.

The story of Rick starting his own leadership journey

My first leadership role was in Newton, Iowa, when I became Executive Director of the Chamber of Commerce.

It was a two-person shop. It was me and one other person. In that situation you pretty much do everything. I had never really managed anyone before, like as a supervisor or manager. With one person, you don't get to do a lot of managing. You both do everything, so what needs to happen is clear. It was a great experience being in that role because I learned that I'm not a maintainer. My first thought was, "How do I build this organization? Fix it? Get it to grow?" It's just natural.

In that role, we did a lot of new programing and new services. It's amazing when I think back about how many things we did for people. My staff member handled all the administration of things: the receptionist, the bookkeeper, the secretary. Any of the programing, I did; I ran the board of directors, and every single program you actually have to create and deliver. One of my big accomplishments was starting a leadership program from scratch, which later become known as Leadership Newton.

One key thing I learned that has helped me in every role since was that when I have an idea for something, I try to find other people that have the right experience or share the vision that would be able to help guide me. So I'll use Leadership Newton as an example. There was a program called Leadership Iowa, and it was a statewide leadership development program. When I had the idea of creating a local one – because I knew other communities had local leadership programs – I went to the roster of local people who graduated from

Leadership Iowa. I did that because they will get the vision quickly because they know what I'm talking about. I created a committee of people that were all graduates of Leadership Iowa, and they helped build out the curriculum for Leadership Newton. It was less about planning things and more about finding resources to do the things I knew would bring value to our members.

Diana J. Wong, PhD
CEO & President
of Sensei Change
Associates, LLC

Diana is a strategy consultant and executive coach for transforming organizational change and leadership careers. As an Associate Professor in Strategic Management and Organization Development, Diana teaches and conducts research in strategic management, entrepreneurship, organization change, leadership development, and international management at the College of Business at Eastern Michigan University. She also leads a highly diverse and multi-lingual global team who delivers engagements around the world which includes Canada, Mexico, India, China, Belgium, Rwanda, Ethiopia, and the Middle East North Africa (MENA) region.

In strategic consulting engagements, she facilitates strategic planning, consults on organization development and change, designs and delivers management skills training and leadership development, and provides executive coaching. Her strategic planning experience supports corporate clients in automotive, healthcare, professional services, manufacturing, and higher education. Diana engages audiences with a range of purposeful creative large group processes such as open space technology or the unconference model, world café, whole scale

Insights in Leadership

change, liberating structures, and points of you to generate positive dynamic involvement from different perspectives.

Diana provides executive coaching to support leaders in developing competencies that sustain competitive organizational positions. Executive coaching includes leadership development, career coaching, and leading complex collaborative teams. Her consulting experience started in 1989 with the Canadian negotiating team on subsidies for the US-Canada Free Trade Agreement and NAFTA. Due to the increasing client demands, Diana launched Sensei Change Associates, LLC in 2002. She also presents on future-oriented leadership and strategic change topics in various local, national, and international forums to academic, professional, and community audiences.

Education & Post-Doc Training
- 1999, PhD in Strategic Management, University of Massachusetts, Amherst MA, USA

- 1989, MBA in Finance & International Bus., Dalhousie University, Halifax NS, CANADA

- 1985, Graduate Studies in International Development, University of Oslo, NORWAY

- 1982, Bachelor of Home Ec, University of British Columbia, Vancouver BC, CANADA

Professional Certification
- *2015, Certified Linkage Leadership Coaching Program*

- *2010, Certified, Denison Organization Cultural Audit and Leadership Assessment*

- *2006-18, Certified Professional in Learning and Performance, Assoc. Talent Development*

- *2005, Emotional Competence Inventory (ECI) Certification, HayGroup/now Korn Ferry*

Why I asked Diana to share her leadership insights

The reason Diana and I met was a shared passion around helping the people of Michigan recover after the 2008/2009 recession. Without yet knowing Diana, I volunteered to be a speaker and mentor for a program called Shifting Gears. Shifting Gears was a program Diana created to help displaced mid/late career white collar professionals find work in the new economy that was emerging in Michigan during and after the recession. Within that first year of volunteering, Diana offered me one of the lead facilitator roles for the Shifting Gears program. As part of the Sensei Change team, I worked closely with Diana and an amazing group of people she had assembled to do some really trailblazing and important work. It was personally a transformational part of my life and career, and Diana played a key role in that. I asked Diana to contribute because she is one of those leaders with a rare combination of patience, drive, directness, kindness, and creativity, and she is skilled at bringing out the best in others. She also put a huge amount of trust in me with a program that was her creation. So much so that in the first session I ever facilitated, she was on a business trip and did not attend. It is a unique leader that is able to spot talent and trust people at the right time, sometimes even before they trust themselves. She is skilled at assessing and cultivating talent, facilitating powerful conversations, and transformational individual and organizational change. I am excited to have Diana's insights woven into the Honest Culture Journey.

The story of Diana starting her own leadership journey
I taught in a boarding school in Papua New Guinea, and as part of that I was responsible for another seven student teachers. In Papua New Guinea, people have to pay tuition to attend secondary. Elementary is free, and they're in the different villages, but the secondary school services the whole province. So there's only one secondary school, and all the kids would come in from grades 7 to 12. In terms of leading the group, it was more focused on understanding the sharing, teaching, pedagogy, and how to manage classrooms. It wasn't the knowledge stuff, but really more about the skills of how to teach, how to deliver lessons more effectively, and also organizing the schedule. One of the greatest annual puzzles was who teaches when, what subjects, in what room? It's like a four-dimensional, multi-day, problem-solving process. You're looking at a staff of about 45, the different rooms, when they would go, and how students would move. It's always about juggling.

It wasn't an official role, but it was the headmaster's responsibility that he got credit for, while I did the work.

Myself, along with a couple of other teachers, would work on this puzzle. Part of the key here is making sure that everyone is happy with their schedule, and that they get to teach what they want to teach. I learned a valuable leadership lesson – oftentimes you can't have everybody get what they want.

Jane Clark
President of the
Michigan West Coast
Chamber of Commerce

Jane Clark has over 30 years of experience in organizational management. She is recognized as a national leader in the chamber of commerce profession, including service on state and national chamber association boards.

Jane is the president of the Michigan West Coast Chamber of Commerce, an organization that was created through the merger of the Zeeland Chamber of Commerce and the Holland Area Chamber of Commerce in September 2012. The Chamber has more than 1,200 members representing 65,000 employees in the greater Holland/Zeeland area. Jane is responsible for developing and implementing the Chamber's multiyear strategic plan and yearly business plan.

In January of 2020, Jane was recognized as one the 50 Most Influential Women in West Michigan by the Grand Rapids Business Journal. She was recognized for her instrumental work as a catalyst for business growth and development, as a convener of leaders and influencers, and as a champion for our thriving community.

Under Jane's leadership, the West Coast Chamber has received numerous accolades.

Insights in Leadership

In 2018, the West Coast Chamber was named Outstanding Chamber of the Year for the State of Michigan by the Michigan Association of Chamber Professionals (MACP). In 2014 and then again in 2019, the organization was awarded a Five-Star Accreditation from the U.S. Chamber of Commerce. This prestigious distinction is awarded to less than 1% of chambers nationwide, and must be renewed every five years. More specifically, of the approximately 7,000 chambers nationwide, only 127 are Five-Star Accredited.

Jane sits on many community-wide boards and committees, including the SARB Board in Downtown Zeeland, the Lakeshore Advantage Board, and the Housing Next Board. She is also a member of Model Communities Initiative and a member of the Riverview Group. Jane is a 1985 graduate of Indiana University and a graduate of Leadership Holland and Leadership West Michigan. She has been recognized as a Certified Chamber Executive (CCE) by the Association of Chamber of Commerce Executives Association.

Why I asked Jane to share her leadership insights
While I have known Jane since becoming a chamber member in 2009, it was working with her during our implementation of EOS that I really got to see her leadership first hand and how it has impacted the community where I live. Since our EOS launch, I have had front row seats to watch the core value of Think Big, Be Great get lived out and raise the bar, and what great actually means.

That is Jane – she is always getting better, and when you are around her it just rubs off. Whenever I am asked to speak or contribute in any way at the chamber I always think, "How can I make this great?", and that is the influence of Jane. Jane is creative, innovative, a creator of memorable experiences, a listener, a connector, courageous, and her influence in the lakeshore community is a testament of her leadership. She also understands her own strengths as a leader, and has learned to bring the right people around her so that she can focus on what she does best and trust the people around her to do the same. I am honored that Jane was willing to share her insights, and I hope her story helps some of you find the courage to try some new things and find the right mentors and coaches along the way.

The story of Jane starting her own leadership journey

I went to school at Indiana University in Bloomington, Indiana. My first real leadership job out of school was in fundraising for the university foundation. I was running their telemarketing program.

My job was to hire and fire college students who would be making calls out to alumni, asking them for contributions to support a capital campaign that the university was doing. One of the key things I remember about that role was hiring. Because they were going to be making telephone calls out – fundraising calls we interviewed them totally over the phone. We would put them in a separate room, and the first half of the interview was all done without seeing the folks. We would bring them in if we could tell that they would be good on the phone and fundraising. If they couldn't talk over the phone to people and have a good conversation, then we'd just say, "Thanks very much. We'll be in touch." If they had potential – if we thought they would be able to ask for the order over the phone, then we'd bring them in and do a one-on-one interview. If they passed the one-on-one interview we would hire them on the spot; we would bring them in, train them up, and put them on the phone.

I also remember that I had no clue what I was doing. I had never supervised people before. Fortunately for me, the university had hired a consultant that did those kind of telemarketing fundraising campaigns all across the country. They had a formula that worked. You followed their formula, and their methodology to raise money. They were very, very good at it.

One of the things I remember is how we would try and motivate these students to get on the phone by having little contests each day. You know, if we raise this much money, then everybody gets back five dollars extra. What went with that – and I was young – was having to let people go who didn't make good fundraisers. That was all a good learning experience.

One of the key lessons I learned that helped me in later sales roles was that you've got to ask for the order. We had clear goals every night. We would know how many calls we were going to try and make and how many connections we were going to get. We would measure, of course, how much in pledges we'd received in individual production goals.

That made managing much easier because if we hired students with a personality for this, and they were competitive, the goals were almost always achieved.

Donna LB Lowry
MD, President/CEO
of Ready for School

Dr. Donna Lowry is the President and CEO of Ready for School. Her vision is that communities will create conditions where all children can thrive and reach their full unique potential. Her leadership role involves multi-sectored, collaborative team building by convening and tracking the community collective in early childhood systems – building, catalyzing, and innovating best practices and ensuring that equity building begins from the very beginning.

As an Obstetrician Gynecologist, Donna's mission to "awaken the possibility of others" has looked like caring for mothers, infants, and coming alongside families with young children. She has practiced in both academic and clinical medicine with the University of Pittsburgh and the Spectrum Health-Michigan State University collaborative. She is a graduate of Hope College, Wayne State University School of Medicine (AOA), the University of Pittsburgh Medical Center, Magee-Women's Hospital, and the University of Michigan School of Public Health. After completing residency in Obstetrics & Gynecology, she concentrated her clinical research interest in Pediatrics & Adolescent Gynecology. Energized by learning, innovation, and their synergy she has completed studies

Insights in Leadership

in the Foundations of Public Health at University of Michigan, is involved with clean water and HIV/AIDS work through Blood: Water Mission, supports the work of Black River Public School, and quality improvements in health care administration.

Donna and David love time with their three sons: Will and Sam, who are studying at the University of Michigan and Harvard respectively, and Jonathan, who is a senior at Black River Public Schools. Together they take in what Great Lakes Lakeshore living offers – great people, sailing, paddle boarding, biking, the arts, and educational travel.

Why I asked Donna to share her leadership insights

A few years ago, Donna called me to connect, share some career thoughts, and get my input. I knew Donna through some common friends, but my first thought was, "Why is an MD calling me for insight and wisdom? What can I offer a smart and accomplished leader like Donna?" (Note the self-doubt cloud forming!) Looking back, that pretty much sums Donna up – humble, smart, confident, resourceful, and introspective. I also cannot think of many people that are so driven by doing good. A year or so after that initial meeting, I had the opportunity to help her implement EOS in her organization, Ready for School. It was in that partnership that I saw more of the same characteristics in Donna that I had seen from the beginning. The one I would add is gracious. I have gotten more pictures, notes, and gifts from Donna than any other leader I have ever worked with. The theme is always reminding me of the impact

I am having on their team, their organization, and the children that they serve. She is a mission-driven leader, and I knew that including her in my list of experts would expand the topic for all of you and help me shift my own perspective – and of course, Donna delivered.

The story of Donna starting her own leadership journey

I took a gap year before I entered medical school. I worked for the Naval Medical Research Institute in Bethesda, Maryland. Though I didn't know at the time, I was working with seven Navy SEALs in behavior modification in an environmental chamber where we would change the temperature. We did cognitive exercises to see how the change of ambient temperature changed their uptake on learning and memory tasks. The Navy SEALs at that time were a secret. There were no movies and no documentaries on these people, but I had to lead them. They put me as the primary point person on this task. It was interesting because I was leading a group of really strong men, and that wasn't something that I was accustomed to doing. I was tasked with leading them through the protocols of the Naval Medical Research Institute, all of the things that they had to sign, and the experiments.

It was a great first leadership role because the why and the what were very clear for our work. We're looking for these specific outcomes that will help you enhance your performance when you're in situations that are really high risk.

As for the team, they were out of their comfort zone because they knew that they were being researched. They were wearing a bathing suit and white socks in a 30-degree environmental chamber doing a memory learning task at the keyboard. Then you would switch them, over the course of two hours, to making it hotbox at 110 degrees. I also didn't have them on a pedestal. I didn't know what SEALs did and was not familiar with the program. So it was just human beings meeting human beings and a task that was important as the United States Defense Department moving from Cold-War-kind-of policy to Desert Storm. Covert operations were moving from one set of realities – from extreme, cold ambient temperature – to really, really hot. The focus was, how can we learn to be better in these environments that we have no control over?

A big takeaway from this experience was that if you have alignment on what you're looking to accomplish, have the right people doing it together, and stay focused on the task, the work gets accomplished.

Javier Olvera
President/Co-Owner,
Olvera Enterprises

As president of Olvera Enterprises, Javier Olvera wears many hats. The company, which he owns with his wife Kerry, his brother Pablo, and his sister-in-law Maricela, runs successful Hispanic grocery stores in Grand Rapids and manages a robust real estate portfolio. As a result, every day is different for Javier, and being motivated by learning, leading, and adapting, he would not have it any other way. It has been his mode of operating since age 16, when he and his family arrived in the United States.

A 2003 graduate of Ferris State University, Olvera's first taste of entrepreneurship came in 1996, when the ownership group purchased La Tapatía grocery store in Grand Rapids. The company later acquired Supermercado Mexico in 2010 and broke ground in 2011 for another Supermercado Mexico. The combined overall growth of Olvera's enterprises has averaged 24 percent per year since 2006. The company employs 75 people across all operations.

These experiences have allowed Olvera the opportunity to learn leadership and people skills that have resulted in creating a family-like culture, and a successful business operation. Olvera credits

Insights in Leadership

his business success to his desire to adapt and learn from others.

"Our culture is one of learning, leading, and adapting. We did not start out as business owners. We had to learn skills and we have continued to help our employees improve on skills. We aim to be resilient and adapt to the world to keep ahead of the curve. We also treat our employees as family. Many of them have been with us for many years," said Olvera when asked to describe the culture of his business.

Some accolades the company has received under his leadership include Supermercado Mexico's numerous 'best workplace' nominations and awards, including Edward Lowe Foundation's 'Michigan Top 50 Companies to Watch' (2013) and West Michigan Hispanic Chamber of Commerce's 'Most Promising Business of the Year' (2012). In 2017, Javier was honored with the prestigious 'Pacesetter Award' from Ferris State University.

Javier is an active community volunteer, having served in volunteer leadership roles at numerous civic and business organizations. Currently he serves as a board member for the City of Grand Rapids' Sister Cities International initiative with Zapopan, Mexico, and as a board member for the Grand Rapids Chamber of Commerce. Javier is also a graduate of leadership programs Elevate and Instituto Crece Latino.

Javier is very well known in the Grand Rapids area, however he is especially recognized as a pioneer in the City's Hispanic business corridor and for his attempts to diversify business ownership in Grand Rapids. "I feel that there is more need to diversify in Grand Rapids and this (active involvement) is one way to accomplish it. For this reason, we are working on creating a destination Mexican Plaza with many businesses and events.

Why I asked Javier to share his leadership insights

I met Javier when he was part of a leadership program launched by the Grand Rapids Area Chamber of Commerce targeted at equipping and elevating minority business leaders. It was appropriately named Elevate. Whenever I speak to small groups, my offer is always to provide some one-on-one time if they have more questions. Most of the time nobody calls, but Javier did. In getting to know him since that time I can see why he called – because he is what we call a growth-minded and open-minded entrepreneur. He is always trying to get better and is willing to ask for and accept help. Add to that an intense desire to lift up the Hispanic community in Grand Rapids through providing jobs, a great culture for his team (he calls them family), and memorable service to all their customers. If you are ever in the Grand Rapids area, I encourage you to stop in to one of the Supermercado Mexico locations and eat something. I always bring home some homemade tamales, and they are excellent! Javier is a pure entrepreneur, in that he walked away from a comfortable corporate job to partner with his wife, brother, and sister-in-law to start a business. He is the only pure entrepreneur on this list, but that is only one of the reasons his voice needed to be in this book. The others are his perspective as a minority business owner, a leader who gets culture and sees it through his unique cultural lens, and finally, he is just a kind person. I am grateful Javier was willing to lend his voice to the Honest Culture Journey.

The story of Javier starting his own leadership journey
While it was not my first leadership role, my leadership journey really started when I became an entrepreneur at 12. I opened and managed my own tire repair shop. My dad helped me lease some space, and I fixed tires for people. I did everything from taking them off the car, fixing them, and then reinstalling them on the car. It's amazing now that I think about it because I was so young, but it felt good.

Years after that experience, it was another entrepreneurial venture when I had my first real leadership role. In 2006, we started Supermercado Mexico. I was part of the leadership team that consisted of my brother, my sister-in-law, and my wife. My unique ability is to create momentum behind new ideas. So my role on the team is more of the visionary. I bring the team new ideas and ask them, "How can we get there?" I also see better ways to do things so I focus energy on how we can make our business more efficient. Finally, I am always looking to the future, and that translates into driving the long-term vision for our organization so we all know where we want to be.

The beginning was a challenge because we were learning the ropes of how the grocery store works. We didn't have anyone that could really guide us in running a grocery store, but we leveraged all the resources that existed and took many classes and workshops to learn things like how to do a balance sheet and how to influence other people. As partners, we were all engaged in the business during our start-up years, and that really helped me develop a deep, hands-on knowledge of the business. That foundation of knowledge really helped as we shifted a couple of years ago to have each leadership team member focus on areas where they have natural strengths. It was at that point I shifted my role to become the visionary of the company.

As a leader, I don't see myself as a person of power who is *in charge of people* in any way. I see my role as helping other people in any way that I can so we can get to where we want to go as an organization. I also see a leader's role as pushing the limits and goals for the organization and providing input and support so we can get to our targets.

Learning has been the key to our success. We have gotten support from a variety of people to help us grow as leaders so we could be successful. More recently, we started working with someone we call an instructor (aka, coach/consultant) that comes from Mexico once a month. He stays with us for the entire week, and during that week, we work on our personal leadership and our teamwork. He challenges us to talk about who's doing what, how everyone is feeling, and what we can improve.

Resources

The Clear Targets Step

- *Traction: Get a Grip On Your Business* by Gino Wickman

  *I have mentioned EOS several times in this book, and it stands for the Entrepreneurial Operating System®. It can be a great tool for the right leader, and I encourage you to read *Traction* and visit *eosworldwide.com* to learn more. Feel free to call me if you have any questions.

- *Get A Grip: How To Get Everything You Want From Your Entrepreneurial Business* by Gino Wickman and Mike Paton

  *Explains EOS in a fable format about a company that might resemble yours.

- *Can You Say What Your Strategy Is?* by David J. Collis and Michael G. Rukstad (Harvard Business Review)

- *Building Your Company's Vision* by James C. Collins and Jerry I. Porras (Harvard Business Review)

- *Joy, Inc.: How We Built a Workplace People Love* by Richard Sheridan

- Contact Diana Wong at Sensei Change Associates *(senseichange.com)*

The Conversations Step

- *Crucial Conversations: Tools for talking when the stakes are high* by Kerry Patterson, et. al.

- *Fierce Conversations: Achieving Success at Work and in Life, One Conversation at a Time* by Susan Scott

- *Leadership and the One Minute Manager* by Ken Blanchard

- *Radical Candor* by Kim Scott

- *For Men Only: A straightforward guide to the inner lives of women* by Shaunti and Jeff Felhahn

- *For Women Only: A straightforward guide to the inner lives of men* by Jeff and Shaunti Felhahn

The Pause Step

- Read the book *Traction* and focus on Chapter 8, the Traction Component™

- *Dare to Lead* by Brené Brown

- *Crucial Conversations: Tools for talking when the stakes are high* by Kerry Patterson, et. al.

- *Fierce Conversations: Achieving Success at Work and in Life, One Conversation at a Time* by Susan Scott

- *Death by Meeting* by Patrick Lencioni

- *Radical Candor* by Kim Scott

Made in the USA
Monee, IL
06 December 2020